LUX CHRISTI

LUX CHRISTI

AN OUTLINE STUDY OF INDIA

A Tmilight Land

CAROLINE ATWATER MASON

GYAN

Published by

GYAN

Gyan Publishing House
5, Ansari Road
Daryaganj, New Delhi-110002
Phone: 011-47034999, 9811692060
E-mail: books@gyanbooks.com

Distribution Network
gyanbooks.com
India, USA, Canada, UK, Australia, France

ISBN: 978-81-212-8468-4 (PB)
First Published, 1902

2nd Impression 2023

Printed at: Gyan Press, Delhi.

LUX CHRISTI
Author: CAROLINE ATWATER MASON

LUX CHRISTI

THE ANGEL OF CAWNPORE

LUX CHRISTI

AN OUTLINE STUDY OF INDIA

A Twilight Land

BY

CAROLINE ATWATER MASON

New York
THE MACMILLAN COMPANY
LONDON: MACMILLAN & CO., LTD.
1903

STATEMENT

OF THE CENTRAL COMMITTEE ON THE UNITED STUDY OF MISSIONS

It is well known to many friends of missions that one of the results of the Ecumenical Conference of Foreign Missions in 1900 was a movement for a system of united study among all the women's foreign missionary societies in the world.

During the year 1902 the plan has been tried and proved most successful. The first course in the regular series was introductory and historical, concerning the progress of missions from apostolic times to the close of the eighteenth century, and was entitled "An Introduction to the Study of Missions." The general idea and the special topics have been taken up with great and unexpected enthusiasm in nearly all of the forty women's foreign missionary societies in the United States and in Canada, and in some societies in Great Britain. The text-book for the course, "Via Christi," has reached a sale of thirty-five thousand copies, and testimony as to the value and interest of the course has been almost universal.

The Central Committee now present as the second course in the series, for 1903, "A Study of India," for which "Lux Christi" is the text-book. India is a fascinating country to study, and encouraged by past success this second outline and text-book are sent out with great confidence in their cordial reception.

Miss A. B. CHILD, Chairman,
704 Congregational House, Boston, Mass.

Miss CLEMENTINA BUTLER,
Secretary and Treasurer,
Newton Centre, Mass.

Mrs. J. T. GRACEY,
177 Pearl Street, Rochester, N.Y.

Miss ELLEN C. PARSONS,
Presbyterian Building,
156 Fifth Avenue, New York City.

Mrs. N. M. WATERBURY,
Tremont Temple, Boston, Mass.

PREFACE

THE foundation of the United Study of Missions was laid by Miss Hodgkins in "Via Christi." It is fitting that the next subject of study should be India, for two reasons: India was the first field of Anglo-Saxon Protestant Missions, and by reason of the seclusion and oppression of its women, it is preëminently woman's foreign missionary field. It can be said without hesitation that no portion of the heathen world can offer us a more fruitful subject for study and investigation, whether we regard the kinship of the great Aryan race, the romance and adventure of early missionary history, or whether we consider the land itself, with its wealth of ancient literature, profound philosophy, and wonderful architecture; with its story of dramatic conquest and its haunting sense of mystery.

The present position of India as a dependency of our Anglo-Saxon kinsmen brings it peculiarly within the range of our interests; its prominence in the fiction of the day brings it vividly before our imaginations. May God grant that a year of earnest study shall lay the burden of its Christless millions heavily upon our hearts.

In "Lux Christi" the author seeks to furnish simply a starting-point from which students may work out in all directions into the rich store of literature accessible. The little book is an outline, not a picture; a condensed summary, not a history of India, religious, political, or social. Neither is it a study of Christian missions in India in detail. To enter in any real sense upon that undertaking would require a series of volumes, and but a portion of two chapters was available. The attempt has been made to give the master motives, major powers, and great historical workers their fitting place; only a few words, however, could be allowed to each, and many worthy names have been of necessity omitted altogether. Technical terms have been avoided and accents on Indian words have been omitted lest their use should add to the unfamiliar and difficult aspect of the pages.

The author's thanks are especially due to Miss Child, Mrs. Gracey, and Mrs. Waterbury of the Central Committee for invaluable aid in the preparation of this study, and also to many other friends who have helped with timely suggestions; in particular Dr. J. T. Gracey and Dr. T. S. Barbour. During the progress of this work numbers of reports, tracts, periodicals, and books, as well as letters, have been received from all parts of the country, from Canada, and also from England, Scotland, and Sweden. All have concerned India and all have been of interest and value. It has been impossible to acknowledge these favors individually, or to incorporate in "Lux Christi" a fractional part of their important information. May this means be taken for cordial thanks for these welcome aids. They have served a purpose, perhaps, above and beyond what was hoped for by those who sent them, for they have furnished a revelation of the magnitude of the work of God in India, and of the devotion of workers of every name. They have furthermore offered convincing evidence of the insignificance of the divisive differences between Christians, of the greatness of the underlying unity. Too long have we confined ourselves to the detailed study of our own limited fields, missing the sweep and the thrill which come with the wider knowledge of the work of the

Church Universal. Nothing, in its way, could be more broadening and illuminating, or more full of encouragement than a systematic study of the work in India of *all* Christian missions. To this end the author would request that some effective method of exchange of periodical and other denominational literature appropriate to the general theme shall be devised, in order that each may know all, and that we may see henceforth not Methodist India, or Presbyterian, or Baptist, but *Christ's India*.

C. A. M.

BATAVIA, N. Y.,
July 6, 1902.

CONTENTS

V

VI

APPENDIX

India lies
mainly between paral-
lels 10° and 40°, the Tro-
pic of Cancer bi-
secting it. It is cross-
ed by two great mountain
systems; the Himalayas,
the highest in the world, and
the Vindhyas. Mt. Everest, consecrated
to the god Siva and his wife, Parva-
ti, is the highest peak of the Hima-
layas: North of the Vindhyas the
central plain is known as Hindustan;
the vast plateau south as the Deccan. The
Deccan is skirted on its west (Malabar) and east
(Coromandel) coasts by mountain ranges known as Ghats (steps).
The chief rivers of Hindustan are the Indus, Jumna, and Gan-
ges; of Burma, the Brahmaputra and Irrawaddy; of the Dec-
can, the Godaveri and Krishna. The Narbada is sometimes
counted the dividing line between North and South India.
The extreme length and breadth are equal, 1900 miles.
The area is as large as that of Europe save Russia. Pop.
288,000,000 Climate tropical in general. Culti-
vation of crops and irrigation of land
wholly dependent on monsoon which
brings rainy season from July to
September. Fauna and flora
those of both temperate and
tropic zones. Chief products,
rice and other grains,
sugar, cotton, opium,
indigo, spices, Cal-
cutta the Capital.
Wonders of ar-
chitecture: Taj Ma-
hal, etc. at Agra and
Delhi; Caves of El-
lora; great Tem-
ples of Cudda-
lore, Tanjore,
etc.
in South
India.

TABLE I

Development of Hindu Religions

1500 B.C.–1900 A.D.

First Period. — Vedism, 1500 B.C. to 900 B.C.

Age of the Vedas. Chief gods, Varuna, Agni, Surya, Indra, Ushas, Yama, Rudras, Soma. All natural forces. Worship chiefly chanting and thank-offerings of rice, soma, and clarified butter. Non-idolatrous. Mention made of thirty-three gods in the Vedas. Woman held in high esteem.

Second Period. — Brahmanism, 900 B.C. to 1200 A.D.

Rise of the power of the priesthood, of the systems of animal sacrifice, and of caste. The Brahmanas, Code of Manu, Upanishads, and Sutras, the Great Epics, and the Puranas produced.

Third Period. — Buddhism, 543 B.C. to 900 A.D.

Growth so great that in 250 B.C. Buddhism was declared the state religion of India. During the ninth century A.D. it was driven out of the peninsula by a Brahmanical uprising. Survives chiefly in Ceylon and Burma. Jainism is a survival of Buddhism.

Fourth Period. — Modern Hinduism, or popular Mythological Brahmanism. This phase had its rise about 400 B.C., coincident with rise of Buddhism, and has continued down to the present.

Idolatrous worship of the Triad, — Brahma, Vishnu, and Siva, their wives, and of Krishna, Rama, Kali, etc. Thirty-three millions of deities. Dogmas of transmigration, caste, and Brahman dominance fixed and universal. Worship of demons, spirits, serpents, the cow, the ox, and the bull, the fish, tortoise, and bear (the last three as incarnations of Vishnu), of plants, of the symbols of generative energy (Linga and Yoni). Fetish worship. Degradation and seclusion of women.

LUX CHRISTI

CHAPTER I

THE DIM CENTURIES

Here sits he shaping wings to fly;
His heart forebodes a mystery;
He names the name Eternity.

Heaven opens inward, chasms yawn,
Vast images in glimmering dawn,
Half shown, are broken and withdrawn.
— TENNYSON.

IN the period during which the Hebrew people, led by Moses out of Egyptian bondage, were wandering on their devious course northward, or were entering their Promised Land by the fords of the Jordan, another great exodus was taking place, nearly two thousand miles to the east.

Where the Caucasus and the Himalaya ranges meet, and the Oxus and the Indus have their sources, lies a vast and lofty ridge known as "the roof of the world." Here dwelt a people of the great Aryan race, proud, free, and conscious of their strength, who found their land too narrow for their vigorous growth.

The Indo-Aryans

Led by their seers (Rishis), chanting the earliest hymns of the Vedas, this mighty conquering horde poured southeastward through the rugged passes of the Caucasus and the Himalayas and entered their Holy Land, the Land of the Five Rivers (now known as the Punjab). Delighted with the wealth of rivers, the newcomers named their new land India, for the river Indus, or Sindhu.

Great Asia wears as a belt around her body, from the Red Sea to the Amoor River, a zone of desert plateau, studded here and there along its lower line by mountain ranges. Hanging like three trophies from this belt are three great peninsulas. Of these three, the central and greatest is the mighty pendant of India, "great, gray, formless India."

Between the Himalayas and the Vindhya mountains stretches the great central plain of Hindustan. The tribes which now pushed their way through this plain eastward toward the Jumna and the Ganges were not a nation of newly emancipated serfs, like the Hebrews, neither were they, like them, of Semitic origin (descendants of Shem, first-named son of Noah). They belonged to the splendid Aryan stock, from which the Brahman and the Englishman alike descend. From one and the same root spring the Celts, the Goths, the Slavs, the Persians, and the Hindus, all tracing their common origin to Japheth. The name "Aryan" means "noble"; the word "Sanskrit," descriptive of the stately language of the Indo-Aryans, signifies "polished."[1] They were a highly intellectual people, subtle and profound, poetic and religious in their instincts, skilled in logic, and, even in those shadowy ages, already achieving some skill in astronomical and other science. In person they were handsome, tall, fair, fine-featured, full-bearded. Valiant in war, full of energy and force, these primitive invaders of India are shown by the Vedas to have had high conceptions of family and domestic life; marriage was sacred among them and women held a high position. "Husband and wife were both rulers of the house and drew near to the gods together in prayer."

Aborigines of India

Like the Hebrews on their entrance into Canaan, the Indo-Aryans, on their victorious march, found it necessary to conquer the aborigines, the native dwellers in the land. These non-Aryan races of India were of a distinctly lower type than their conquerors, dark-skinned, flat-nosed, squat in figure. They are described in the Vedas scornfully as "disturbers of sacrifices," "raw-eaters," etc. They designated them the "Dasyus," or enemies, and the "Dasas," or slaves. These lower tribes be-

[1] The Sanskrit is no longer a spoken language.

longed to three great roots known as the Tibeto-Burman, the Kolarian, and the Dravidian. The descendants of the first-named are still to be found in the foot hills of the Himalayas, chiefly in upper Burma and Assam; the second are now scattered through central India; while the Dravidians are to be found quite compactly in the south.

Each of these three groups has given rise to a large number of native, non-Aryan dialects. Out of twenty belonging to the Tibeto-Burman group we may mention the Burmese, Naga, and Garo; out of nine Kolarian dialects, the Santali is the chief; the Dravidian tribes furnish twelve distinct languages, among which are Telugu, Tamil, and Kanarese. The greater portion of these aboriginal tribes have submitted to the conquering race, and the mixed descendants of conquerors and conquered now make a large part of the Hindu people. About an equal number of each race have kept their ancient stock comparatively pure. There still linger, in the jungles and mountains, remnants of still earlier aboriginal tribes than these mentioned, for the latter seem to have been themselves invaders of India in some dim, prehistoric past.

Contrasted Development of Hebrews and Indo-Aryans

We have begun this study by drawing a parallel between the contemporaneous exodus of two great peoples, the Hebrew and the Hindu. We mark that at the outset the Indo-Aryans were a free, highly developed people, entering a vast and fertile continent; while the Hebrews were a horde of slave-born wanderers, taking possession of a rocky strip of coast. The question must arise, Why should the Jewish people have advanced in civilization, intellectual force, and in spiritual attainment so far beyond the Hindu? The answer may be briefly given as geographical and religious. India lies largely within the tropics. The enervating tropical climate has produced in the course of centuries a dreamy and brooding mental habit in place of the early creative and aggressive energy. Palestine, lying well to the north, bred a hardier and more stubborn type of men.

The Hindus assimilated the semi-civilization of Asia; the Jews the culture of Greece and Rome and of modern Europe.

Israel with its lofty, original Jehovistic faith, which was destined indeed to be —

> " dipt in baths of hissing tears,
> And battered with the shocks of doom,"

yet in the end rejected every form of pagan polytheism, and thus by its unique monotheism became the channel through which the Supreme Revelation of the one God could logically come. The religion of the Indo-Aryans, on the other hand, while starting with a comparatively pure nature-worship (although the Rig-Veda has allusions to thirty-three deities), rapidly degenerated into ritualistic and mythological Brahmanism with its monstrous misconceptions and puerile superstitions. With the degeneration of its religion has come the degeneration of the people.

The story of ancient India is in the main the story of the rise and fall of its religious systems, as the Hindus, in spite of an enormous bulk of literature, have no history, no records, no annals, for a reason we shall find later.

I. THE HINDU RELIGION, MARKED BY THREE DISTINCT PHASES

1. Vedism.

Going back to dim pre-Vedic ages, *i.e.* the ages before the Vedas were known, we find the first conception of Deity among the Aryans to bear the name Varuna, "the Encompasser," the name given to the infinite vault of heaven — not to the sky, the realm of cloud and wind and rain. The hymns addressed to Varuna which survive in the Vedas are not only the earliest contained in them and the noblest, but they are apparently monotheistic, although this monotheism was quickly lost. What in the Vedas often appears monotheistic, *i.e.* the ascription of supreme attributes to some Deity, is in reality due to the practice of worshipping *one god at a time*, and seeking to propitiate him by exalting him as the One and Only.

The primitive objects of worship in the absence of revealed religion are sure to be the forces of nature. Such were the gods of the Aryans, known under the general name of Devas, "the bright ones." Agni, the god of fire, Indra, the god of rain, Surya, the sun or god of day, constituted a trinity of divinities. The Sun-god was also worshipped as Mitra, and the three letters, A. U. M., which combine to form the mystic syllable Om, were originally the initial letters of the trinity composed of Agni, Indra,[1] and Mitra.

This notion of a triad, indefinitely multiplied, runs throughout the whole Hindu religion. The Vedas speak of the gods as "thrice eleven" in number, while later ages give thirty-three millions.

To the trinity of Fire, Wind, and Sun were soon added Ushas, the Dawn; Yama, the King of Death; Rudras, the Storm God or Destroyer; and Soma, the Deification of the exhilarating juice of the soma plant. The Ninth Book of the Veda, composed of one hundred and fourteen hymns, is wholly devoted to the praise of soma. Indra was supposed to be peculiarly addicted to the intoxicating draught, and he is thus addressed in the Rig-Veda, "Indra, take into thy belly the full wave of the inebriating soma, for thou art lord of libations." Again, with scant ceremony, "Sit down, Indra, upon the sacred

[1] Varuna (U) was sometimes substituted for Indra.

grass, and when thou hast drunk the soma, then, Indra, go home." Great were the orgies of gods and men on the Indian Olympus! Agni, the Fire-god, was especially pleased by offerings of clarified butter (*ghee*), as the pouring of this substance upon fire produced a brilliant blaze. The favorite epithets for Agni were therefore "butter-haired," "butter-backed," etc.

The Vedic religion, in place of the stoical pessimism of later Hinduism, was full of a "joyous sense of life." The Rig-Veda has not a little poetic fire and elevation. Suggestions are found in it of the common traditions of the Creation, the Fall, the Deluge. The Vedas give no sanction to the doctrine of transmigration of souls, the burning of widows, the prevalence of child-marriage, the tyranny of caste (explicitly), nor the practice of idolatry. But while they are free from many of the corruptions of decadent Brahmanism, "they will be found," says Monier Williams, Boden Professor of Sanskrit at Oxford, "when taken as a whole, to abound more in puerile ideas than in lofty conceptions." Max Müller, the first translator of the Vedas, says, "Large numbers of the Vedic hymns are childish in the extreme"; sentiments and passions unworthy of deity are ascribed to the gods, not one of whom indeed, save Varuna, is of a pure and lofty character. Intelligent modern Hindus do not conceal their own disappointment at the sterility of the Vedas, which for centuries were practically unread. In short, the time has gone by for enshrouding these interesting memorials in imposing mystery, and seeking to overawe the uninitiated by assertions of their inconceivable grandeur. They are translated now and can be read by any one who has patience to push his way through the "unarranged, promiscuous mass . . . destitute of system or harmony." Here and there may be found a noble hymn, a lofty prayer; but between these oases are illimitable deserts of tedious sensuality, fantastic and monotonous beyond belief. The claim of extreme antiquity for the Vedas is surpassed by that of the earlier Hebrew scriptures; and the moral elevation of the latter, as well as their sustained poetic grandeur, shine with peculiar lustre by comparison.

Vedism, or the purer early religion of the Vedas with its underlying monotheism, may be said generally to have extended to the eighth century B.C., when it was gradually overgrown by the second phase of Hindu religion, Brahmanism.

2. **Brahmanism.**

This word is formed from the term "Brahma," signifying the Supreme Soul of the Universe, at first known as *Atman*, the Breath of Life.

The priestly class had now gained great power, and in their hands the Vedas were interpreted to suit their own ends. The vague suggestion of caste in the celebrated Purusha[1]

[1] See pp. 31–32 for the origin and significance of caste.

hymn of the Rig-Veda was by the priests or Brahmans developed into a fourfold order, an unparalleled social tyranny. The Brahmanas, or ritualistic treatises, "which have hardly their match for pedantry and downright absurdity," were added to the Vedas, and the sacrificial system, which fed the priesthood more than the gods, was enormously elaborated, so that "the land was deluged in the blood of slain beasts."

The Code of Manu

The Code of Manu, although of gradual growth and indefinite date, belongs to this epoch. It came into being to stem the tide of rationalistic thought to which the exaggerations of the sacrificial system had given rise. This Code stands for rigid conservatism, for the iron severity of caste, and for the *lex talionis* in bitterest cruelty, as thus indicated, "With whatever member of the body a low-born man may injure his superior, that very member of his body must be mutilated." (Book VIII.) "A once-born man insulting twice-born men with abusive language must have his tongue cut out." (Book IX.) The authors of the Code of Manu were evidently Brahmans, and its undeviating purpose is to intrench the Brahman caste finally and forever in its authority. The superiority of the Brahmans is the hinge on which the whole social organization turns. Besides these doctrines the Code of Manu discourses largely on the transmigration of souls. The following, in brief, is this theory, which is important as being a pervasive, practical force to-day in all Hindu life and thought, as characteristic of Buddhism as of Brahmanism :—

Every act and every thought produces either good or evil fruit. As a result of conduct on earth the spirits of men are reincarnated in an endless succession of forms. The accepted number of rebirths is 8,400,000. A common colloquialism for the attainment of salvation is "*to cut short the* 84." A threefold alternative is presented to the soul : it may pass through deities, through men, or through beasts and plants. It will go through deities if goodness prevails in its nature ; through men if it is ruled by passion ; through beasts and plants if it dwells still lower in the moral scale, as, for instance, the soul may be reborn in the form of a worm in the body of an unclean beast.

A Brahman, neglecting his own appointed caste duty, will be born as a vomit-eating demon ; a soldier, as a demon feeding on excrement and dead bodies ; a husbandman, as a demon feeding on putrid carrion.

The deterioration of the Vedic writings is well illustrated by comparing these degrading and loathsome terrors with the calm repose and noble faith of the Burial Hymn.[1]

[1] p. 32.

The Ninth Book of the Code of Manu relates to women and fixes their status of inferiority and subservience as we find it in India to-day.

"Women have no business with the text of the Veda; this is fully settled; therefore having no knowledge of expiatory texts, sinful women must be as foul as falsehood itself. This is a fixed law," etc. Hindu cosmogony and cosmography are dealt with in the code in a manner equally intelligent.

Systems of Philosophy

As an outgrowth of the rationalistic tendency which the Code of Manu was framed to meet, we find at about this time a body of speculative doctrine put forth called the Upanishads. The dread of continued passing from one form of life to another had become "the one haunting thought which colored the whole texture of Indian philosophy." To liberate the spirit of man from this bondage of transmigration was known as "the Way of Knowledge," and constituted "the *summum bonum* of Brahmanical philosophy."

Upon the Upanishads are built the three ruling systems of Hindu philosophy, viz., Nyaya, Sankhya, and Vedanta. The last named is the leading philosophy of India. The name means "the end or scope of the Veda." Its two cardinal principles are Illusion — Maya

— and Pantheism. Maya is "a play which the Absolute plays with himself." The "great saying" is *Om*, i.e. *I am God* or *I am He*. Again, "The whole universe is God." "There is nothing else." "Ignorance makes the soul think itself different from God, and it also *projects* the appearance of an external world," in short, the finite world with all its appearances is all illusion.

We can now understand why the history of the Hindu people has never been written or preserved. Vedantic and other similar doctrine have so practically and universally permeated the popular mind with the conception that all is illusion, that no human being and no earthly events or conditions have the slightest value, or are in any way worthy of record or investigation.

Pantheism

Pantheism, the theory that all is God and God is all, — there is nothing real in the universe but God, for God *is* the universe, — lies at the foundation of every phase of Hinduism, and expresses itself in the polytheism which regards all things, from the soul of man to the blade of grass, as *worshipable*, since all alike are pervaded by divinity. Even the most uneducated Hindus state that they are themselves parts of the Deity, as are all other beings in the universe. This cardinal doctrine is summed up in the Chandogya Upanishad, "*This atom belongeth to the Over-Soul, is the All, is the Truth, is the Over-Soul. That art thou.*" The lack of a sense of sinfulness, characteristic of the people, finds here its obvious explanation. There can be no guilt where all that we call good or evil is but the *necessary* self-manifestation of the one unconscious essence. All that we behold or conceive, — animals, men, natural forces, and gods, — are, according to the theory of Brahmanism, alike divine. Hence the rapid multiplication of deities to thirty-three millions in decadent Hinduism.

Reaction under Gautama

In the sixth century B.C. there was born the son of a rajah of the Sakya tribe of Aryans, named Gautama, and afterward called the Buddha, or Enlightened One. Of the religion which was founded by this remarkable reformer, we shall speak more fully later. We mention it at this point only to consider its effect upon Brahmanism, against the tyranny and exaggerations of which it was a noble protest and one which for a time bade fair to prevail.

Wherever the new religion spread, it produced a profound revolution in Indian thought and was enthusiastically accepted. With marvellous adroitness and subtlety the Brahmans met this reaction ; proved themselves able to assimilate all that they chose of the new cult, to popularize new aspects of ancient gods and heroes, and to weave all into one vast system, known as Hinduism, the lineal descendant of Vedism and Brahmanism.

"Like an immense glacier," says Rowe, "slowly descending from the mountain, gathering up and incorporating stones, earth, and débris of whatever kind comes in its way, but at the same time accommodating itself to the configuration of the mountain side, so has Hinduism come down through the ages, gathering up and incorporating whatever gods and goddesses, heroes and saints, religious theories and doctrines, rites and ceremonies, came in its way. So flexible is Hinduism, and in a certain way so tolerant, that Christianity, its deadly foe, could at once be incorporated into this huge system if Christians would but consent to have Jesus Christ regarded as one of the innumerable gods of the Hindu pantheon, form a caste subdivision by themselves, and pay proper homage to the Brahmans."

3. Modern Hinduism or Mythological Brahmanism.

Buddhism grew to a great popularity in the century after the death of its founder, and it appears to be coincident with this movement that the Brahmans began to popularize their own religion, and to seek to satisfy the craving of the people for personal gods with human attributes. Thence proceeded the gross degeneration of Hinduism, *i.e.* mythological Brahmanism. The system is briefly this: the prime universal essence is Brahmă (neuter), which when united to Maya, or Illusion, gives birth to the primeval male god, Brahmā, the Creator of all inferior forms, from himself to a tuft of grass. Two other essential functions, Preservation and Destruction, made it necessary to associate with Brahma two other personal deities, — Vishnu, the Preserver, and Rudra-Siva, the Dissolver and Reproducer. These three gods, concerned in the threefold operation of integration, maintenance, and disintegration, constitute the *Tri-murti*, or Sacred Triad of decadent Brahmanism. Of these three Brahma is practically ignored in the popular mind, and the original spiritual essence is lost in the very earthly personalities of Vishnu and Siva.

Hindu Tri-murti

A Hindu poet of the third century A.D. thus idealizes the unity and the equality of the *Tri-murti*: —

> "In those three Persons the one God was shown —
> Each first in place, each last, — not one alone;
> Of Brahma, Vishnu, Siva, each may be
> First, second, third, among the blessed Three."

From a work on India, by W. G. Williams, we take the diagram here given of the three members of the *Tri-murti* and their wives: —

Brahmă, the Supreme
Maya — Illusion

Brahmā, Creator, and Sarasvati, his wife.	Vishnu, Preserver, and Lakshmi, his wife.	Siva, Destroyer, and Parvati, his wife.

Parvati, wife of Siva, is also known as Durga and Kali. Her son is Ganesa, the elephant-headed god of wisdom, who is, moreover, a great glutton, devoted to soma and pancakes. The whole pantheon, indeed, teems with horrible and grotesque creations, half monster and half god.

Vaishnavism

While each of the three persons of the *Trimurti* has its own proper following, Vaishnavism, the especial worship and exaltation of Vishnu, the Preserver, has the popular heart.

The chief distinction of Vishnu is that he has condescended to infuse his essence at different times into animals and men, in a series of descents or incarnations, known as avatars. The ten great avatars are: 1. The Fish. 2. The Tortoise. 3. The Boar. 4. The Manlion. 5. The Dwarf. 6. Rama with the axe. 7. Rama-candra, the hero of the Ramayana. 8. Krishna, the most popular, and perhaps the most demoralizing, of all the Hindu gods. 9. Buddha (adopted as an avatar of Vishnu, according to some authorities, in a spirit of shrewd compromise; according to others, as a

Lying Spirit let loose to deceive men until the final descent of Vishnu). 10. Lalki. This descent, which is the last, is reserved for an indefinite future, when the wicked shall be destroyed and the world renovated.

It is needless to attempt to enumerate the later Hindu gods and goddesses. They range from varying conceptions and expressions of the universal essence to the most loathsome fiends and ogresses.

Kali Worship

The female principle is worshipped under countless forms. The most appalling conception is that of Kali, who is thus described in the Tantras, or sacred books of Goddess-worship: "One should adore with liquors and oblations that Kali, who has a terrible gaping mouth and uncombed hair; who has four hands and a splendid garland formed of the heads of the giants she has slain and whose blood she has drunk," etc., *ad nauseam.* Says a Hindu gentleman: "Popular ideas on the subject of Kali-worship by no means reach the mysterious vileness it suggests. Its real meaning cannot be explained. Those inclined to dive into such filth must study the ritual for Kali-worship."

Decline from Varuna to Krishna

Place beside this hideous distortion the figure of Krishna, the grossly immoral, coarse, and low-minded cowherd whose cult was worked out in the sixth century of the Christian era, and which is now the popular religion of India. Then glance back to the "roof of the world," and see the steady road of decadence and degeneration by which Hinduism has travelled from the free, high-hearted, conquering Aryans with their worship of the pure, all-encompassing infinitude of Varuna. Nevertheless the seed was in itself, for a taint of polytheism resided in the earliest Vedic conceptions of deity, — a taint which, in the course of ages, has poisoned the blood in every minutest vein of the great Hindu organism.

This third and worst stage of Hinduism is now the religion of probably over two hundred and seven millions of souls in India, to which it is confined, since Hinduism is essentially an ethnic religion, like Confucianism and Zoroastrianism.

II. BUDDHISM

We have spoken, on an earlier page, of the birth of Sakya-Muni, or Gautama, the Buddha, or Enlightened One, in the sixth century B.C. Space cannot be given in this study to a detailed account of his life and teaching. The main events and features are easily accessible, and as Buddhism is not an accepted or established religion at the present time in peninsular India, its detailed consideration belongs elsewhere.

The legends narrate that Gautama, son of a rajah of the Aryan race, born at Kapilavastu, in northern India, thwarted his father's desire for his worldly pleasure and advancement by his meditative and ascetic habit. Finally, at the age of twenty-nine, he broke away from the court altogether, and made what is known as his "Great Renunciation," forsaking his palace, father, wife, child, and assuming the dress and entering upon the life of a mendicant.

For six years Gautama practised the austerities of a Brahman ascetic, but found no peace. Then he returned to the ordinary life of common people, and after sitting lost in contemplation under the sacred pipal tree at Gaya for a week and suffering from divers fiery temptations, he attained to the vision of the Way of true peace and holiness. After this experience Gautama was known as the Buddha.

Buddhist Doctrine

Although he broke with the current Brahmanism of his day at many points, Buddha remoulded without discarding its most monstrous fiction, viz., the transmigration of souls. This doctrine, indeed, in a somewhat idealized form, was the essential foundation of his whole system. Starting with the conviction that the delusion of individuality is the chief Fetter of the soul, and the désire for preserving the identity, the promoting cause for the myriad rebirths, Buddha sought and found "the Way" to the only release, the only salvation, *i.e.* Nirvana, literally the "going out," as of the flame of a candle.

The Buddhist books (the Tripitaka, three baskets) are full of descriptions of means by which to get rid of the delusion of individuality, to enter the Path to Extinction. The conception of moral discipline, love, charity, and fraternity, as "the Path," in place of sacrifice and ceremony, is the nobly distinguishing note of Buddhism in contrast with Brahmanism. For polytheism, the Buddha substituted atheism, without however breaking sharply with the established system. He never claimed divinity, and was a saviour only in that he taught his rules for perfection, which were an immense advance over the teaching of Brahmanism, but far below the level of the teachings of Christ. He died of indigestion at Kusinara, at the age of eighty years.

Spread of Buddhism

Buddhism was from the first a missionary religion, unlike Brahmanism, which has never gone beyond India. Multitudes accepted its teachings in Nepaul, Thibet, Burma, Ceylon, China, Siam, and Japan, and it is now the popular religion of all eastern Asia save India, numbering four hundred millions of adherents. In India the new religion in a few centuries largely took the place of Brahmanism, being zealously promulgated by the renowned Indian monarch, Asoka, the Constantine of Buddhism. Asoka even sent missionaries to Syria, Egypt, and Greece to proclaim the doctrines of Buddha.

Buddhism driven out of India

In its turn Buddhism, however, became enfeebled and corrupt. After a fierce struggle, confused and protracted, against the rehabilitated Brahmanism, with its tempting array of social and dramatic deities, it was annihilated in India, save as absorbed into the great Hindu system. Its monasteries and temples were destroyed, its priests and people slain, exiled, or brought over to the ancient faith.

Burma and the island of Ceylon are the only parts of India where Buddhism now lingers. In them both, Buddhism in its purest and least adulterated form can be found. The latter is the seat of Buddhist scholars and devotees. At Kandy is the temple in which is preserved the so-called "tooth of Buddha," the object of intense adoration. Buddhism survives also to a certain extent in southern India in the form of Jainism, which is a product of mixing Brahmanism and Buddhism. Its temples are particularly noteworthy. Together Buddhism and Jainism number a little more than seven millions of the population of India.

Defects of Buddhism

It is noticeable that to no one of the nations professing it has Buddhism given advanced civilization or a high type of personal religion. Its theories are lofty but singularly barren, as are all stoical systems. It has been common of recent years to refer to Arnold's "Light of Asia" as an authoritative utterance concerning Buddha. That perfervid piece of hero-worship, however, bears slight resemblance to the simple dignity of the real story of Gautama, and is looked upon by philosophical Buddhist scholars as a species of metaphysical Lalla Rookh. It may be added in passing, concerning the cult known in England and America as "Esoteric Buddhism," that Dr. Rhys Davids, our chief authority on the religion of Gautama, says it may be all very well, but it is not esoteric, and it is not Buddhism.

The Pitakas have not all, as yet, been translated. When complete they will cover ten thousand pages. They are said to be turgid and wearisome in the extreme.

Much as it has been vaunted by recent enthusiasts, early Buddhism was atheistic, and it remains a gloomy religion, bloodless and lifeless, and has become grossly degraded by superstition. Says James Freeman Clarke: "It is an outward constraint, not an inward inspiration. Nihilism arrives sooner or later. God is nothing, man is nothing, life is nothing, death is nothing, eternity is nothing. Hence the profound sadness of Buddhism. . . . The only emancipation from self-love is in the perception of an infinite love. Buddhism, ignoring this infinite love, incapable of communion with God, aiming at morality without religion, at humanity without piety, becomes at last the prey to the sadness of selfish isolation. . . . Christianity touches Buddhism at all its good points, in all its truth. . . . but to all this it adds how much more! It fills up the dreary void of Buddhism with a living God. . . . It gives a divine as real as the human, an infinite as solid as the finite. And this it does, not by a system of thought but by a fountain and stream of life."

THE SACRED LITERATURE OF THE HINDUS,

to all of which the inclusive term Veda (Divine Knowledge) is applied by the Brahmans. The original text of all is Sanskrit, but many parts have been translated into the Vernacular.

I. The four Vedas proper.

While existing orally for many centuries before Christ, these productions remained unwritten until the fifteenth century A.D.

The four books are each divided into two parts: first, the Mantra, or hymns of praise and prayer; second, the Brahmana, a ritualistic treatise, generally in prose, somewhat akin to the book of Leviticus in the Hebrew Scriptures.

1. *The Rig-Veda, or Hymn-Veda.* This is the first Bible of the Hindu religion, the oldest and only important part of the four Vedas. It is a collection of 1017 hymns, containing 10,580 verses, chiefly addressed to the gods. It is the great literary memorial of the entrance of the

Aryan race into India, about 1500 B.C. It shows them on their victorious march through Cabul to the Punjab, among the great river systems of the Indus and the Jumna, and moving eastward to the Ganges.

2. *The Sacrificial-Veda, or Yahur-Veda,*[1] belongs to a later phase of the Hindu system, and is mainly liturgical.

3. *The Chant-Veda, Sama-Veda,* closely resembles the second. It contains hymns to be chanted at certain ceremonies where the juice of the soma plant was the chief offering.

4. *The Spell-Veda, Atharva-Veda,* is much later in origin than the rest, and was not perhaps recognized as a fourth Veda until about the fifth century B.C. The most prominent characteristic feature of the Atharvan is the multitude of incantations which it contains.

II. The Code of Manu.

Date, about 600 B.C. according to Monier Williams.

The body of Hindu law, whose originator is unknown. It is the chief authority in Hindu jurisprudence, and contains precise rules for the constitution of the Hindu social fabric, for the due coördination of its different orders, and for the regulation of everyday domestic life.

These rules are contained in three principal codes which together constitute a kind of Bible of legal Brahmanism, and remain, in their control of Indian social and domestic life, little changed by the lapse of more than two thousand years. The rules of caste are rigidly enforced.

Book I is on Creation. Book II on Education and the

[1] A few years ago a part of the Yahur-Veda was translated into the Vernacular for general circulation. Cautious as is the British government in offending the religious prejudices of the people, those concerned in the translation and publication were punished as having violated the law against obscene literature.

Priesthood. Books III–IV on Private Morals. Book V on Diet. Book VI on Devotion. Book VII on the Duties of Rulers. Book VIII on Civil and Criminal Law. Book IX on Women, Families, and the Law of Caste. Book X on Mixed Classes and Times of Distress. Book XI on Penance and Expiation. Book XII on Transmigration and Final Beatitude.

III. The Upanishads and Sutras.

Date, about 500 B.C.

The Upanishads, or "instructions," formed the Bible of philosophical Brahmanism. At least two hundred and fifty of them are known to exist. They had their origin in the ascetic tendency which led many Brahmans to flee to the forests for seclusion in which to pursue their flights of speculative thought. These recluses gradually composed and built up a series of forest treatises known as the "Aranyakas," out of which grew the later and more systematized Upanishads. The systems of philosophy which are founded on these mystical and speculative writings are known as Shastras, a term which is also used to cover the Vedas and the whole body of laws, letters, and religion. The Sutras are concise sentences which contain "the distilled essence of all the knowledge which the Brahmans have collected during centuries of meditation."

IV. The two great Epic Poems, the Ramayana and the Maha-bharata, which may be called "the Bible of the Mythological Phase of Brahmanism."

Date, variously placed from 500 or 400 B.C. to the beginning of the Christian era.

These two poems are called "The Iliad and Odyssey of the Hindus," and there is some reason to believe that the motifs of them were borrowed from Homer.

The Ramayana, sometimes termed "The Iliad of the

East," treats of a war undertaken to recover the wife of one of the warriors, who was carried off by the hero on the other side. Rama is the hero; the chaste and beautiful Sita, his wife. The poem consists of twenty-four thousand verses.

The Maha-bharata is the most gigantic poem in existence, containing two hundred and twenty thousand lines, and is not a single poem, but an unwieldy collection of Hindu mythology, legend, and philosophy. Different portions can be traced to different dates.

Included in the great epic is an interpolation known as the Bhagavad-Gita, or "Divine Song," consisting of a long discourse in dialogue form by Krishna. It affirms the divinity of Krishna, and is an attempt to reconcile the various Hindu philosophies. It is usually assigned to the third century A.D.

V. The Puranas.

Date, 600 and 700 A.D., and later.

The name Purana signifies an old tradition. These, the most modern of Hindu sacred books save the Tantras, are sometimes called a fifth Veda, being designed to teach Vedic doctrines to women and low caste men. The theology and cosmogony of these books are largely drawn from earlier writings. As far as actual history or chronology goes, the Puranas are valueless, but their myths and legends shed light on the customs of the people and times. Contending sects have contributed to them many absurd fictions for the glorification of Vishnu, Siva, and other favorite deities. The Puranas contain one million six hundred thousand lines, and may be called the Bible of Saivism and Vaishnavism.

VI. The Tantras.

Date not fixed, probably somewhat later than the Puranas.

The Bible of Saktism, inculcating exclusive adoration of Sakti, wife of the god Siva. The Tantras present

Hinduism "at its worst and most corrupt stage of development." They identify all force with the female principle in nature. "A vast proportion of the inhabitants of India are guided in their daily life by Tantrik teaching and are in bondage to its gross superstitions." (Monier Williams.) The Tantras have never been translated.

FAMOUS PASSAGES FROM HINDU LITERATURE

Hymn to Varuna

Let me not yet, O Varuna, enter into the house of clay; have mercy, almighty, have mercy!

If I go trembling, like a cloud driven by the wind, have mercy, almighty, have mercy!

Through want of strength, thou strong and bright god, have I gone to the wrong shore; have mercy, almighty, have mercy!

Thirst came upon the worshipper, though he stood in the midst of the waters; have mercy, almighty, have mercy!

Whenever we men, O Varuna, commit an offence before the heavenly host; whenever we break thy law through thoughtlessness; have mercy, almighty, have mercy!

—*Rig-Veda.*

Hymn of Creation

In the beginning there was neither naught nor aught;
Then there was neither sky nor atmosphere above.
What then surrounded all this teeming universe?
In the receptacle of what was it contained?
Was it enveloped in the gulf profound of water?
Then there was neither death nor immortality;
Then there was neither day, nor night, nor light, nor
darkness,
Only the Existent One breathed calmly, self-contained.

Naught else but he there was — naught else above, beyond.
Then first came darkness hid in darkness, gloom in
 gloom;
Next all was water, all a chaos indiscrete,
In which the One lay void, shrouded in nothingness.
Then turning inwards, he, by self-developed force
Of inner fervor and intense abstraction, grew.
First in his mind was formed Desire, the primal germ
Productive, which the wise, profoundly searching, say
Is the first subtle bond connecting Entity
And Nullity. — *Rig-Veda.*

How many births are past, I cannot tell;
 How many yet to come no man can say;
But this alone I know, and know full well,
 That pain and grief embitter all the way.
— *South India Folk Song.*

A Brahman who holds the Veda in his memory is not culpable though he should destroy the three worlds. — *Code of Manu.*

THE PURUSHA HYMN

The embodied spirit has a thousand heads,
A thousand eyes, a thousand feet, around
On every side enveloping the earth,
Yet filling space no larger than a span.
He is himself this very universe;
He is whatever is, has been, and shall be;
He is the lord of immortality.
All creatures are one-fourth of him, three-fourths
Are that which is immortal in the sky.
From him, called Purusha, was born Virāj,
And from Virāj was Purusha produced,
Whom gods and holy men made their oblation.
With Purusha as victim they performed
A sacrifice. When they divided him,
How did they cut him up? What was his mouth?

What were his arms? and what his thighs and feet?
The Brahman was his mouth, the kingly soldier
Was made his arms, the husbandman his thighs,
The servile Sūdra issued from his feet. —*Rig-Veda.*

This hymn (generally admitted to be a comparatively modern production) is the only hymn in the Rig-Veda which alludes to the distinctions of caste.

As set forth in the hymn the divine order of caste seems to be :—

1. The Brahman, who is supposed to issue from the mouth of Brahmā. The Brahmans are therefore regarded as divinities, whose teaching is an infallible authority. They only can teach the Veda.

2. Kshatriya, or the "kingly soldier," who issues from the arms of Brahmā. This caste ranks next the Brahmans in position and influence, coöperating with them in retaining ascendency over the lower classes. To it belong the famous Rajputs.

3. The Vaisya, or husbandman caste, which comes from the thighs of Brahmā. To this caste belong endless subcastes according to kind of occupation. These three ranks claim to be "twice born," and are all invested with the sacred thread, which is of cotton for the Brahmans, hemp for the Kshatriya, wool for the Vaisya.

4. The Sudra, or servile class, issuing from the feet of Brahmā, comprising those only "once born."

All below the Sudras are *outcaste*, or Pariahs.

The Sudra and the unmarried woman of any caste, even the highest, are left outside the pale of Brahmanical salvation.

Burial Hymn

Open thy arms, O earth! receive the dead
With gentle pressure and with loving welcome.
Enshroud him tenderly, even as a mother
Folds her soft vestment round the child she loves.
Soul of the dead, depart! take thou the path—

The ancient path by which our ancestors
Have gone before thee; thou shalt look upon
The two kings, mighty Varuna and Yama,
Delighting in oblations; thou shalt meet
The Fathers and receive the recompense
Of all thy stored-up offerings above.
Leave thou thy sin and imperfection here;
Return unto thy home once more; assume
A glorious form.

— From the *Sutras*.

Simple Confession of a Vedantist's Faith

All this universe indeed is Brahma; from him does it proceed; into him it is dissolved; in him it breathes. So let every one adore him calmly.

— *Chandogya Upanishad*.

Moral Precepts

An archer shoots an arrow which may kill
One man, or none; but clever men discharge
The shaft of intellect, whose stroke has power
To overwhelm a king and all his kingdoms.

— *Maha-bharata*.

Do naught to others which, if done to thee,
Would cause thee pain; this is the sum of duty. — *Ibid*.

When men are ripe for ruin, e'en a straw
Has power to crush them like a thunderbolt. — *Ibid*.

Enjoy thou the prosperity of others,
Although thyself unprosperous; noble men
Take pleasure in their neighbor's happiness. — *Ibid*.

An evil-minded man is quick to see
His neighbor's faults, though small as mustard-seed;
But when he turns his eyes toward his own,
Though large as Bilva fruit, he none descries. — *Ibid*.

Treat no one with disdain, with patience bear
Reviling language; with an angry man
Be never angry; blessings give for curses.
— *Code of Manu.*

The soul is its own witness; yea, the soul
Itself is its own refuge: grieve thou not,
O man, thy soul, the great internal witness. — *Code.*

Thou canst not gather what thou dost not sow,
As thou dost plant the tree so will it grow. — *Code.*

He who by firmness gains the mastery
Over his words, his mind, and his whole body,
Is justly called a triple governor. — *Code.*

'Tis a vain thought that to attain the end
And object of ambition is to rest.
Success doth only mitigate the fever
Of anxious expectation; soon the fear
Of losing what we have, the constant care
Of guarding it, doth weary.
— *Hindu Drama, Kalidasa.*

The most prolific source of true success
Is energy without despondency. — *Ramayana.*

Where'er we walk, Death marches at our side;
Where'er we sit, Death seats himself beside us;
However far we journey, Death continues
Our fellow-traveller, and goes with us home. — *Ibid.*

Opinion of an Expert

After a life-long study of the religious books of the Hindus I feel compelled to express publicly my opinion of them. They begin with much promise amid scintillations of truth and light, and occasional sublime thoughts from the source of all truth and light, but end in sad corruptions and lamentable impurities. — SIR MONIER WILLIAMS.

THE BUDDHIST PATH OF SALVATION

And if you should ask, "How does he who orders his life aright realize that Nirvana?" I should reply: "He, O King, who orders his life aright grasps the truth as to the development of all things, and when he is doing so he perceives therein birth, he perceives old age, he perceives disease, he perceives death; but he perceives not therein, whether in the beginning, or the middle, or the end, anything worthy of being laid hold of as lasting satisfaction. . . . And discontent arises in his mind when he thus finds nothing fit to be relied on as a lasting satisfaction, and a fever takes possession of his body, and without a refuge or protection, hopeless, he becomes weary of repeated lives. . . . And in the mind of him who thus perceives the insecurity of transitory life, of starting afresh in the innumerable births, the thought arises: All on fire is this endless becoming, burning, and blazing! Full of pain is it, of despair! If only one could reach a state in which there were no becoming, *there* would there be calm, *that* would be sweet — the cessation of all these conditions, the getting rid of all these defects (of lusts, of evil, and of Karma), the end of cravings, the absence of passion, peace, Nirvana!"

And therewith does his mind leap forward into that state in which there is no becoming, and then has he found peace, then does he exult and rejoice at the thought: "A refuge have I gained at last!" — RHYS DAVIDS' "Buddhism."

ATHEISM OF BUDDHA

I do not see any one in the heavenly worlds, . . . nor among gods or men, whom it would be proper for me to honor. — BUDDHA.

THEMES FOR STUDY OR DISCUSSION

I. The Aryans and the Native Tribes of India.
II. The Rig-Veda.
III. Contrast between Judaism and Hinduism.
IV. The Rivers and Mountains of India.
V. Pantheism and Polytheism.
VI. The Great Epics of India; Comparison of these with the Iliad and the Nibelungenlied.
VII. The Weakness and Strength of Buddhism.
VIII. What Influences have led to the Decadence of the Hindu People?
IX. Hindu Symbols, Gods, and Images.
X. Caste, the Supremacy of the Brahmans, and the Transmigration of the Soul, the Cardinal Points of Hinduism.
XI. The Hindu Triad: Brahma, Vishnu, Siva, with the Incarnations of Vishnu.
XII. Buddhist and Jain Architecture.

BOOKS OF REFERENCE

For general reference on this and succeeding chapters:—

Bliss's "Encyclopædia of Missions."
Reclus's "India and Indo-China," Vol. III, in "The Earth and its Inhabitants."
"Encyclopædia Britannica," article "India," by Sir W. W. Hunter, or its equivalent, "The Indian Empire," by the same author.
Hunter's "Brief History of the Indian Peoples."
Gracey's "India."
Beach's "Cross in the Land of the Trident."

For special reference on above themes:—

Butler's "Land of the Veda," II, VIII, IX, X.
Clarke's "Ten Great Religions," II, III, V, VI, VII, IX, XI.

Rhys Davids' "Buddhism," VII.
Fergusson's "Indian Architecture," XII.
Graham's "Great Temples of India, Ceylon, and Burma," XII.
Kellogg's "Handbook of Comparative Religions," V, VI, VII, VIII, XI.
Living Papers Series, "Non-Christian Religions of the World," I, II, V, VII, VIII, IX, X, XI.
Max Müller's "Origin of Religion," II, V.
Max Müller's "India and what it can teach us," II.
Max Müller's "Chips from a German Workshop," II, VII.
Ragozin's "Vedic India," I, II, V, VI, XI.
Reed's "Hindu Literature," II, V, VI, VIII, IX, XI.
Rousselet's "India and its Native Princes," IV, IX, XII.
Sir M. Williams's "Indian Wisdom," II, V, VI, X.
Sir M. Williams's "Religious Thought and Life in India,"[1] II, V, VIII, IX, X, XI.

[1] A later edition has been published under title "Brahmanism and Hinduism."

DATES FOR INDIA'S POLITICAL HISTORY

508 B.C. .	Persian Invasion under Darius.
327 . . .	Greek Invasion under Alexander the Great.
316 . . .	Chandra Gupta founds Behar.
250 . . .	Asoka establishes Buddhism as state religion.
161 . . .	Bactrian Invasion.
100 B.C. –500 A.D.	Scythian or Tatar Invasions.
700 A.D.	Earlier religions merged in Modern Hinduism. Parsi settlements in western India.
1001 . . .	First Invasion of Punjab by Mahmud of Ghazni.
1000–1765	Mohammedan Invasions and rule of Islam.
1398 . . .	Tamerlane invades India.
1525–1857	Mughal Empire.
1556 . . .	Akbar the Great, } Famous Mughal rulers.
1605 . . .	Jehangir, } Famous Mughal rulers.
1627 . . .	Shah Jehan, } Famous Mughal rulers.
1658–1707	Aurangzeb, } Famous Mughal rulers.
1498 . . .	Portuguese Expedition under Vasco da Gama.
1500–1600	Portuguese Monopoly of Oriental trade.
1602 . . .	Dutch East India Company founded.
1604 . . .	The French enter India.
1600–1857	British East India Company maintains military and commercial power.
1739–1761	Afghan Invasion and Sack of Delhi.
1757 . . .	Lord Clive's victory at Plassey establishes British Empire in India.
1857 . . .	Sepoy Mutiny and Dissolution of East India Company.
1877 . . .	Queen Victoria proclaimed Empress of India.

CHAPTER II

INDIA'S INVADERS

For the gods —
They smile in secret, looking over wasted lands,
Blight and famine, plague and earthquake, roaring deeps
and fiery sands,
Clanging fights and flaming towns, and sinking ships and
praying hands. — TENNYSON.

WE now emerge from the dusk of legend and tradition into the light of written history.

For the facts of India's authentic history we must, however, turn to foreign writers. While from them we learn of many successive invasions marking many phases of national life, we can, broadly speaking, divide the whole history into three great eras: the Hindu, the Mohammedan, and the British.

I. PERSIAN INVASION

In the year 508 B.C. Darius Hystaspes, successor of Cyrus the Great, is said to have undertaken an expedition against India. He caused a fleet to be fitted out upon the Indus, under the command of Scylax, who pushed his way into the Punjab, and by his conquests added an immense revenue to the Persian treasury. Later we hear of Indian soldiers, clothed in white cotton, marching in the ranks of Xerxes' army against the Greeks.

II. GREEK INVASION

In 327 B.C. Alexander the Great invaded India, by way of Afghanistan, and conquered Porus, the Indian ruler of the sacred "land of the five rivers," the famous Punjab. Many garrison stations founded by Alexander are to-day prosperous cities, — as Patala (Hyderabad in Sind), Taxila (Deri-Shahan), Alexandria (Uchch), and others. The Greek Megasthenes has left glowing record of the valor of the Indian men and the chastity of the women. Near the close of the fourth century B.C. the native Indian prince, Chandra Gupta, known to the Greeks as Sandracottus, began to build up a rival principality at Behar, in the valley of the Ganges, while the Greek supremacy still existed in the Punjab, and diffused Greek influences which proved to be of a lasting character. The buildings of the Indian people had hitherto been of wood, and destitute of architectural pretension. A new and enduring architecture now succeeded.

Culmination of Buddhism

In the year 260 B.C. Asoka, grandson of Chandra Gupta, ascended the throne of Behar. He ardently espoused Buddhism, and proclaimed it as a state religion. He caused many monuments to be set up bearing Buddhistic inscriptions, some of which, in the form of pillars, are still to be found at Delhi, Allahabad, and at Babra.

Buddhism reached its culmination in India in the seventh century A.D. Its downfall followed soon.

III. MOHAMMEDAN INVASION

Passing over the Bactrian and Scythian invasions, which took place during the period between 161 B.C. and 500 A.D., we now come to the Mohammedan period, which begins in 664 A.D. with the first appearance in the Punjab of the armies of the Crescent. This was but thirty-two years after the death of the Prophet. One Afghan invasion followed another with little result until the reign of Sultan Mahmud, the "idol-smasher," whose name is still illustrious throughout Asia, although he was but the monarch of the petty kingdom of Ghazni. He led seventeen raids into India, finally subduing the Punjab, which he annexed to his own province of Ghazni, and which thenceforth became Mohammedan. Mahmud came to the Mussulman throne in 997 A.D., and reigned thirty-three years. His fame among Mohammedans rests not alone upon his conquests, but upon his greatness as a champion of the faith and as a patron of learning. Mohammed of Ghor at his death, 1206, left all northern India under the rule of Mohammedan generals. His Indian viceroy, Kutab-ud-din, proclaimed himself sovereign of India at Delhi, and founded the dynasty of the "Slave Kings," he having started in life as a Turki slave. His fame is preserved by the wonderful Kutab Minar, the tapering, sculptured shaft on the plain of Delhi.

The Rajputs

In the struggle with the Mussulman power in eastern India a valiant part was played by the warrior chiefs of pure Aryan descent known as the Rajputs, who, when conquered, withdrew to the regions bordering on the eastern desert of the Indus, and founded the province of Rajputana, south of the Punjab. These proud, hereditary chiefs, who could trace their ancestry unbroken to the Vedic age, defied the invaders of their country with stubborn courage, but in vain.

The Mohammedan power grew and spread until, about 1320, it was extended through the Deccan, and all India was practically tributary to it, although its power was never so firmly planted in the south as in Hindustan. The native Hindus yielded reluctantly and slowly to the fierce proselyting of their conquerors, and never gave more than a nominal allegiance to Islam. Indeed, Aryan ideas and customs not only resisted Mohammedan influence more successfully than those of any other Asiatic race, but in the end Mohammedanism has become Hinduized in a marked degree.

IV. TATAR INVASION

About the end of the fourteenth century a number of internal revolts had weakened the power of the Afghan kings of Delhi, and prepared the way for the success of another great invasion. In 1398 Timur, or Tamerlane, with a wild horde of Tatar tribes, swept down through the northwest passes of Afghanistan across the Punjab toward Delhi. His terrific, scourge-like descent, in which fire and sword consumed everything in his way, passed, leaving little permanent result. Late in the preceding century large numbers of Mughals (originally *Mongols*), who had unsuccessfully invaded the Punjab, had become subject to the Delhi kings, and been converted from their Tatar rites to Islam. These foreigners in India furnished the foundation upon which, in the sixteenth century, the great Mughal Empire was built. Babar, descendant of Tamerlane in the sixth degree, in the year 1526 repeated his invasion, and with the help of his followers and of resident Tatars established the Mughal (Mogul) Empire, with its seat at Agra.

The Grand Mughals

The famous Mughal dynasty, which like those preceding it was Mohammedan, covered a period of three hundred and thirty years, ending in 1857 with the banishment of its last representative. The greatest name among its emperors is that of Akbar the Great, grandson of Babar, who died in 1605 and is buried in a magnificent mausoleum near Agra. Contemporary with the reign of Elizabeth of England, the reign of this Indian emperor was enlightened and progressive and offers much of picturesque interest to the student of history. Shah Jehan's reign was the climax of Mughal magnificence. Delhi and Agra were his favorite seats; at the former he placed his famous peacock throne; at the latter that consummate flower of Indian architecture, the Taj Mahal, the mausoleum of his favorite wife. The Taj, which has been described as a dream in marble, an edifice designed by Titans and finished by jewellers, was twenty-one years in building, during which time twenty thousand men were employed on it. The eyes of the architect who designed it were put out by the despotic emperor that he might never design another which could equal or surpass it. It cost over eight millions sterling. The reign of Aurangzeb, son of Shah Jehan, from 1658 to 1707, is the culmination of Mughal power and the beginning of its decay. Even to-day, in British India, official reports are wont to go back to the time of Aurangzeb. Romantic subjects for study are furnished by noted Mohammedan princesses, from Nur Mahal, the Light of the Palace, wife of Jehangir, and the adored wife and beautiful Christian daughter of Shah Jehan, down to the Rani of Jhansi, who fought with matchless valor against the British in the Mutiny of 1857, and died in battle at the head of her troops.

Among the great events which contributed to the disintegration of the Mughal Empire during the lifetime of Aurangzeb and a little later, were the descent of the Afghans under Nadir Shah, their Persian conqueror, in 1739; the formation of the Mahratta confederacy in the Deccan, and the uprising of the Sikh sect in the Punjab.

Sack of Delhi

Six times the Afghans swept down upon northern India with fearful massacres, returning through the famous Khyber Pass with booty amounting to thirty-two millions sterling, plundered during a fifty-eight days' sack of Delhi. The borderland between Afghanistan and India was ravaged and swept bare of inhabitants by these bloody and furious invaders.

The Mahrattas and Sikhs

The Mahrattas (also spelled Maratha) and Sikhs remain to-day prime forces to be reckoned with in the administration of Indian affairs. The Mahrattas are a low caste Hindu race found in the region southeast of Bombay. Although rude in their civilization, they were fierce and formidable fighters. At this period their power rose enormously in the Deccan, and their generals carved out kingdoms for themselves from the decaying empire of the Mughals. To this day the Mahrattas have not forgotten the power they held a century ago, and they have never become reconciled to British dominion.

The Sikhs, unlike the Mahrattas, are not a race, but a religious sect bound together by military organization and discipline. The name Sikh signifies disciple. They trace their origin to Nanak Shah, a Hindu reformer born near Lahore in 1469. Successive religious teachers, known as Gurus (equivalent to the Hebrew Rabbi), inculcated Nanak's doctrine of the abolition of caste, the unity of the Godhead, and the obligation of living a pure life. The ninth Guru in the Sikh succession attracted the attention of the Emperor Aurangzeb, who was himself a fanatical Mussulman. He imprisoned the Guru and tortured him so cruelly that the sufferer prevailed upon a fellow-prisoner to put him to death. Instead of checking the Sikh movement, the murder of the ninth Guru was the great turning-point in the history of the sect. Thenceforward the Sikhs became an organized, compact legion, sworn to die fighting in defence of their faith. "From Puritans they turned to Ironsides, praying and fighting with equal fervor."

The Sikhs now number over two millions, scattered throughout India, especially in the British army. Their religion has degenerated into a hybrid between Hinduism and Mohammedanism, with the Granth, their sacred book, as an idol. Amritsar, their sacred city, is famous for the Golden Temple, where this book lies on its silken cushions, ever surrounded with prostrate adorers. The warlike character of the Sikhs, and the key-position on the borders of the British Empire which they occupy, have led to a firm belief in many quarters that "the fate of British India is bound up with that of the Sikhs."

Last of the Mughals

To return to the Mughals: "The gigantic genius of Tamerlane," says Butler, "and the distinguished talent of the great Akbar, with the magnificent taste of Jehan, have thrown a sort of splendor over the crimes and follies of the great Mughals." . . . Bloody and barbaric despots were they at best. The last of the dynasty, Bahadur Shah, was discovered by the British in 1857, after the fall of Delhi, in hiding, "seated under a small tattered canopy, his person emaciated by indigence and infirmity, his countenance disfigured by the loss of his eyes, and bearing marks of extreme old age and settled melancholy."

He was exiled as a state prisoner to Rangoon, and fills an unknown grave.

The downfall of the Mughal Empire ended the political power of Islam in India, but the king of England in his Indian Empire to-day rules over one-third of all the followers of Mohammed in the world. The fierce and resentful haughtiness of most Mussulmans in India shows that they cling to the memory of their seven hundred years of rule in the land before the hated English came and overthrew their power. The Hindus rather welcomed this event than otherwise, as the rule of the Mohammedans had been bitterly cruel and oppressive, and they had never amalgamated with the conquered people.

Islam

A brief survey of the religion of Mohammed must be taken at this point.

Here we have to do with the most modern of all the religions which can be called world religions, for the date of Mohammed's birth is placed at 570 A.D. and of his flight to Medina (the Hegira) at 622. It is substantially true that Islam is little else than a spurious form of Judaism borrowed from Jewish exiles, with such modifications as suited it to Arabia, plus the important addition of the prophetic mission of Mohammed, and the consuming lust of conquest. The Koran, which takes the place of the Hebrew Old Testament, is a rather poor performance as a Bible, rhetorical rather than poetic, ranking perhaps with the Apocryphal books of the Old Testament Canon.

Mohammed and the Koran

Mohammed, a camel-driver of Mecca, was from his birth a victim to epilepsy and hysteria, the paroxysms of which contributed greatly to his success in an age when such seizures were looked upon as supernatural possession. He early began to have visions of angels, especially of Gabriel, who communicated supposedly divine truth to him in a miraculous manner,—communications usually accompanied by convulsions on the part of the Prophet. In this way, little by little, the Koran was made up, and it is the medley which we might expect.

Dictated from time to time by Mohammed to his disciples, it was by them either treasured in their memories, or written down on shoulder-bones of mutton or on oyster shells, on bits of wood or tablets of stone, which, being thrown pell-mell into boxes and jumbled together, were never arranged until after the Prophet's death. The one hundred and fourteen suras, or chapters, of which the Koran consists, are now placed in the order of their respective lengths, —the longest first, the shortest last: an arrangement as simple as it is illogical. Each sura begins with the words, "In the name of the merciful and compassionate God."

Persecuted and hated by the ruling tribe in his native city, Mecca, there is reason to suppose that Mohammed, at this period of his life, was a sincere though morbid fanatic. No imagination could have dreamed of the tremendous success which was so near at hand. His followers were few and insignificant.

Medina

Medina, north of Mecca, in the same province of Hedjaz, chanced to be at the time a centre of numerous and powerful Jews, who were habitually looking forward to the coming of a prophet like Moses. Mohammed, whose religion at this time was a kind of modified Judaism, with its teachings continually drawn from the Old Testament and the Talmud, perceived the fact that Medina offered a strategic point for the culture of a new religious movement, which should appeal to Jews as founded upon their own Scriptures, and non-idolatrous, and at the same time make proselytes among idolaters, as the Jewish religion could not do by reason of its exclusive rites of circumcision, etc.

The Hegira and Moslem Conquest

To Medina, therefore, on the 20th of June, 622 A.D., the prophet betook himself, preceded secretly by his disciples in small parties.

From this day, the day of the Hegira, the Mohammedan era dates.

Success was sudden, almost miraculous; but as his fortune rose, the character of Mohammed sank in the scale. Cruelty, passion, and plunder now became the rule of life with him and his followers; the prophet was lost in the merciless military conqueror. It has been well said that Mohammed's only element of greatness was success.

In eighteen years all Syria, with Jerusalem,

Damascus, and Aleppo, had fallen before the Mussulman, and Egypt and Persia were conquered. All history presents no movement so dramatic, so startling, so appalling even, as the Saracen uprising.

The followers of the Prophet, coveting the death in battle which exalted them to martyrdom and a sensual paradise, were fired by a fanatical courage which made their onward course for a time irresistible. In Europe, the firm resistance of Charles Martel, in 732, at Tours, turned the tide back upon Asia. In western Asia, Islam has held its own through many centuries; but as its extension is wholly dependent upon military conquest, it has been checked where this has ceased.

It has been claimed that the spread of Mohammedanism in India is far more rapid than that of Christianity; but, in point of fact, its growth there is very slow, as it only keeps pace with the general increase of population.

Characteristics of Religion of Mohammed

It can be said in favor of Islam that it is a great advance upon Brahmanism and Buddhism, in that it holds neither pantheism, polytheism, atheism, nor idolatry; that it is minus the unwholesome tendencies of caste, of a corrupt priesthood, and of a belief in transmigration of souls. The Mussulman believes in one God, even Jehovah; but his monotheism is "the worst form of monotheism which has ever existed"; and, it may be added, his religion presents the most unbroken front to Christianity which it anywhere encounters. The follower of the Prophet is forbidden the use of wine and the practice of gambling, but polygamy and concubinage are sanctioned explicitly by the Koran, and his life as well as his religion is steeped in sensualism. He is a slave owner and a slave trader; fierce and cruel beyond belief, destitute of charity and good will to men, his prime duty indeed being to slay infidels. Fatalism is woven into the texture of his being. "Thus doth God cause to err whom he pleases, and directeth whom he pleases," says Sura, xx. 4. As "*All is Maya*" (illusion) is the watchword of the Hindu, so "*Kismet*" (it is fated) is the watchword of the Mussulman.

"As a social system," writes Stanley Poole, "Islam is a complete failure; by degrading women it has degraded each successive generation of their children down an increasing scale of infamy and corruption until it seems almost impossible to reach a lower level of vice."

This is the religion which to-day in India stands numerically next to Hinduism, numbering more than fifty-seven million adherents. There are those who prophesy that the twentieth century will witness in India a tremendous struggle between Islam, Buddhism, and

Christianity — the three religions which are striving for universal supremacy, the only religions which are not racial.

The Parsis

The conquering progress of Mohammedanism in the eighth century brought about as one result the immigration to the western coast of India of large numbers of Persians, or Parsis, followers of Zoroaster, driven from their own land by the fiery persecution of the Mussulmans. The descendants of these early colonizers are to be found among the merchant-princes, bankers, and financial operators of Bombay and all India. A financial failure among them is felt on every bourse in Europe. As the religion of Zoroaster, although not an Indian religion, is now professed only by the Parsis of India and their brethren in Persia, we must consider it briefly in this study.

Starting in the Vedic period from the same primitive conceptions of divinity peculiar to the Aryan stock, the religion of the Zend-Avesta (the sacred book of the Parsis) soon diverged widely from that of the Vedas. Each, however, retains much in common with the other. There can be little doubt that Ahura-Mazda, the supreme divinity of the Avesta, was originally one with the Varuna of the Vedas. Indra and Mitra appear in both systems. Both regard fire as divine, dread defilement from contact with the dead, and in both the worship of the soma juice is inculcated. There is, however, despite the superficial resemblances, a profound disparity between Hinduism and Zoroastrianism, so that each can say to the other, "Your gods are my demons." The latter, like Buddhism, is an essentially moral religion; but the method of Zoroaster was an eternal battle for good against evil, that of Buddha a struggle for complete self-effacement. The Parsi religion, let it be remembered, is, in its essence, the religion of Cyrus the Great, of whom the prophet Isaiah makes Jehovah say, "I have raised up one from the north, and he shall come; from the rising of the sun shall he call upon my name." It was the only religion of the ancient world which could be in any real sense called monotheism; and yet it too resolved itself into an indiscriminate worship of natural forces, and especially into fire and sun worship.

The distinguishing theory of the Persian religion is its dualism; its belief in a great Spirit of Good and an equally great Spirit of Evil. In the beginning the Eternal, Supreme, and Infinite One produced these two other great divine beings: the first, the King of Light, is called Ormuzd; the second, the King of Darkness, is Ahriman.

Status of Parsi Women

The Parsi religion commands the especial consideration of women in the home as a religious obligation. Children are the crown of glory, and thus the mother became in the Zend-Avesta the "holy, mystic one," through whom the past, present, and future glory of the father was secured. She was regarded as the "goddess of abundance, the irradiator of hearth and home."

As a consequence of this conception, the Parsi women of India occupy a much more honorable position than either their Hindu or Mohammedan sisters. They are refined and intelligent, and enjoy, indeed, almost as much freedom and respect as do women in Europe.

The number of Parsis now resident in India is not great, probably not more than ninety thousand, but they form, intellectually and morally, a distinctly superior class in the population.

V. EUROPEAN INVADERS

Near the close of the fifteenth century there began a series of European invasions of India, markedly different from those of Persians, Tatars, Afghans, and Arabians. The new invaders came ostensibly for peaceful commerce rather than for bloody conquest, territorial aggrandizement, or political power. Only four hundred years, however, were required from the first of these innocent invasions to reduce all India, from the Himalayas to Cape Comorin, to the position of a dependency of the most remote of these European powers,—a power whose own proper territory is less than that of a single province of Hindustan.

Through the Middle Ages little was known in Europe concerning India. It was regarded as a mysterious mine of fabulous riches and splendor. Certain Italian cities, notably Venice, sustained trade with the far-famed golden land, but it was dimly known to Europe at large, save as some adventurous traveller like Marco Polo returned from it with marvellous tales.

The Portuguese in India

When, in 1492, Columbus sailed from Lisbon, he sailed, not for the purpose of discovering a new continent, but a new route to India. He found America instead. Five years later another adventurous Portuguese, Vasco da Gama, embarked for India, whose western coast he touched after an eleven months' voyage. Like the European explorers who followed him, Da Gama entered India from the south, whereas the military invasions had all been made from the north.

Landing at Calicut, on the southeast coast, the Portuguese found favor with the native prince or Rajah. Returning to his own country after six months, Da Gama bore from him the following letter to his king: "Vasco da Gama, a nobleman of thy household, has visited my kingdom and has given me great pleasure. In my kingdom there is abundance of cinnamon, cloves, ginger, pepper, and precious stones. What I seek from thy country is gold, silver, coral, and scarlet."

For exactly a century, from 1500 to 1600, the Portuguese held a monopoly of Oriental trade, with their seat of power at Goa.

The Dutch in India

The defeat of the Spanish Armada in 1588, by which the Spanish and Portuguese were driven off the seas, changed the current of events, and the Dutch and English soon appeared in Eastern waters to compete for the prizes of Indian commerce. The Portuguese were rapidly driven off the field and expelled from all their Indian territory save an area of one thousand square miles on the west coast. Successive private expeditions were made from Holland to India in the latter years of the sixteenth century, and in 1602 all these interests were merged in the "Dutch East India Company." This was the heyday of Dutch maritime supremacy. At about the date, 1619, when they laid the foundation of the city of Batavia in Java, the seat of their government in the East Indies, the Dutch had discovered the coast of Australia and were founding in North America the city of Manhattan, now New York.

The Dutch remained powerful in India until about 1800, when England won away all their colonies, even Java, which has since been restored, and Holland now controls no territory on the mainland of India.

The French in India

France also was represented. As early as 1604 French companies had been formed and ships sent out to engage in traffic with India, but it was not until 1664 that Colbert, successor to the great Mazarin, succeeded in a scheme for enriching France by fostering her Oriental commerce. A great capitalized company was formed, and an adventurer named Cason was despatched to India as director-general of French commerce. He succeeded in getting a temporary foothold in southern India and Ceylon.

The British in India

It was in the year 1600 that England stretched out a strong hand to grasp her share of the riches of India, and completed the circle of hungry European invaders, who, for a century, hovered around the great passive Indian peninsula, like rapacious birds of prey around some prone and helpless giant. More restrained, better civilized, more humane than the Tatar tribes and the hosts of Islam, the European invaders came to India with motives no less selfish and mercenary, for loveless trade is "only war grown miserly."

Great Britain owes her imperial crown of India in the last analysis to a rise in the price of black pepper in the year 1599. The Dutch, who preceded the English in the spice traffic with India by some years, formed a monopoly on black pepper in the year mentioned, and raised the price per pound from three English shillings to eight.

Origin of the East India Company

"This was too much for the Lord Mayor and merchants of London, who resolved to form an association of their own for direct trade with India, and induced Queen Elizabeth to send Sir John Mildenhall to India by way of Constantinople to the Mughal, Akbar the Great, to secure privileges for the new company. On the last day of the year 1600, in the forty-third year of her reign, Queen Elizabeth signed the first charter creating 'One Body Corporate and Politick in Deed and in Name, by the name of the Governor and Company of Merchants of London trading with the East Indies.'"

The new East India Company's charter provided only "that they at their own Adventures, Costs, and Charges, as well for the Honor of this our Realm of *England* as for the increase of our Navigation and Advancement of Trade of Merchandize with our said Realms and the Dominions of the same, might adventure to set forth one or more Voyages . . . in the Countries and Parts of *Asia* and Africa . . . to the benefit of our Commonwealth."

"A circumstance most flattering to the medical profession," said Sir Henry Halford many years after, "is the establishment of the East India Company's power on the coast of Coromandel, procured from the Great Mogul (Shah Jehan) in gratitude for the official help of Dr. Gabriel Boughton in a case of great distress. It seems that in the year 1636 one of the princesses of the imperial family had been dreadfully burnt, and a messenger was sent to Surat to desire the assistance of one of the English surgeons there, when Boughton proceeded forthwith to Delhi, and performed the cure. On the minister of the Great Mogul asking him what his master could do for him to manifest his gratitude for so important a service, Boughton answered, with a disinterestedness, a generosity, and a patriotism beyond all praise, 'Let my nation trade with yours.' 'Be it so,' was the reply. A portion of the coast was marked out for the resort of English ships, and all duties were compromised for a small sum of money."

From this as a beginning dates the famous career of the Old English Company. In the next twelve years twelve voyages were undertaken, and the envoy of the company was graciously received at the court of the Great Mughal. Soon after important factories were established at Surat, Masulipatam, and Hugli. Surat became the seat of the western presidency and remained so until 1684, when this was transferred to Bombay. Bombay was ceded to the British crown as a part of the dower of the Portuguese princess, Catherine of Braganza, in 1661. The site of Calcutta

(*Kalkatta*, named for a shrine of Kali) was acquired by purchase in 1695.

Holland and Portugal were soon crippled and outclassed by the English in the race. Meanwhile the Mughal Empire was falling to pieces, under puppet kings, successors to Aurangzeb, while the Afghans ravaged it from the north, and on one side the Mahratta power and on the other the Sikhs were closing in upon it. There was small chance to notice the insignificant English traders who were quietly establishing themselves in their three ports, — Madras, Bombay, and Calcutta. The French, meanwhile, held Pondicherry and adjacent territory in the Carnatic.

In 1698 the Old English Company had lost its charter, and in 1702 a new company had been formed known as "The Honorable East India Company."

The French and English remained for a generation trading side by side in south India, both paying rent to the Great Mughal. On the death of Aurangzeb, in 1707, the whole of south India had become independent of Delhi, and numerous semi-independent native states were formed. The Mahrattas, with Poona as capital and residence of the Peshwa, were the dominant power.

Clive and Dupleix

In 1744 war broke out between the English and French in Europe. The governor of Pondicherry, Dupleix, had a secret ambition to found a vast French empire in India. His English rival, Clive, was a young writer in Madras. They took up the cause of their respective nations. Hostilities between the French and English in south India therefore, in which each was supported by different states, continued from 1746 to 1761, when Pondicherry capitulated and the French were victoriously driven out. This, it will be observed, was the time when all the northern lands of the old Mughal Empire lay bleeding under the scourge of the Afghan invasions.

The Black Hole of Calcutta

Meanwhile Clive had gone to England, where he had been made a lieutenant-colonel in the British army and governor of Madras. Returning to India, he landed on the 20th of June, 1756. This was the day of the horrible tragedy of the Black Hole of Calcutta, in which one hundred and twenty-three English men and women, taken prisoners in an attack on Fort William by the native Bengal prince, died in a single night, locked into a stifling garrison prison eighteen feet square.

Clive, in Madras, upon learning of this horror, sailed promptly to the mouth of the Ganges, recovered Calcutta from the natives, and peace might have been established had not the English general, in defiance of the neutrality of Bengal, seized just at this time upon a French settlement. The Bengal government offered battle, and Clive marched out to the grove of Plassey, seventy miles north of Calcutta, and won a great victory which suddenly threw the overlordship of the rich and important province of Bengal into English hands. Thus it came about that "the daring of a merchant clerk made a company of English traders the sovereigns of Bengal, and opened that wondrous career of conquest which has added the Indian peninsula, from Ceylon to the Himalayas, to the dominions of the British crown."

VI. THE BRITISH EMPIRE IN INDIA

The battle of Plassey was fought on June 23, 1757, a date which has been adopted by history as the beginning of the British Empire. By this it is not meant that on this day all India fell under British rule, for not even of the province of Bengal would this have been true. The battle of Plassey does, however, mark the point when the British knew themselves to be in India for conquest as well as for commerce, for empire not merely for trade. Their supremacy in India rests upon the same basis as that of the Moslems and the Mughals, although its results are far more beneficent, viz., the right of conquest, and as such is frankly entered in all official statistics.

Policy of the East India Company

Unlike the followers of Mohammed, however, who nominally subjugated India in the name of the one true God and to spread their religion, Englishmen at this time explicitly forswore all religious motives or proselyting purposes. Up to the time of Clive, the East India Company had tolerated and befriended Christian missionaries. Afterward, as it grew in power and the dream of empire loomed large, its representatives adopted the policy of forcibly keeping Christian missionaries out of the land and encouraging the native idolatries. English soldiers were even obliged at times to make a show of reverence before especially sacred heathen shrines.

Clive and Warren Hastings, at least, were deliberate conquerors, and theirs was no accidental policy when they laid the foundations of England's supremacy amid the chaotic ruins of the last Mughal's empire. They builded no better than they knew. Lord Wellesley (1798–1805) firmly laid down the unchangeable purpose of England to hold complete supremacy in the peninsula, which has inspired all later policy. Circumstances conspired to make the work an easy one. To a great extent the English caused the native factions to do their fighting for them, pitting one against another, and cleverly turning the result to their own advantage.

Progress of Subjugation

"The British won India," says Sir William Hunter, "not from the Mughals, but from the Hindus. Before we appeared as conquerors, the Mughal Empire had broken up. Our final wars were neither with the Delhi king nor with his revolted governors, but with the two Hindu confederacies, the Marhattas and the Sikhs. Our last Marhatta war dates as late as 1818, and the Sikh confederation was overcome only in 1848."

This is a condensed summary of the long wars which followed Plassey. One governor-general succeeded another, each adding territory or strengthening the British government in its foothold. It was not until 1828, when Lord Bentinck came into office, that the nobler conception of a government *for the good of the governed* can be said to have really gained ground. Lord Bentinck's statue at Calcutta bears an inscription from the pen of Lord Macaulay, setting forth the unselfish benevolence of his rule. He suppressed *suttee* (the burning of widows on the funeral pyres of their husbands) and stamped out the horrible practices of the *thugs*. (These were hereditary assassins, who made strangling their profession, travelling in bands, disguised as merchants or pilgrims, and were sworn together by an oath based on the rites of the bloody goddess, Kali, of whom they were devotees.)

The Punjab was annexed in 1849 and Burma in 1852 by Lord Dalhousie, after long and tedious wars running back to 1826, when Assam, which had been seized by the Burman king, was ceded to the British and became a state of India. Lord Dalhousie completed the fabric of British rule in India, finally adding Oudh and Central Provinces, besides many minor states, before his retirement in 1856.

Lord Dalhousie was succeeded by Lord Canning, later known, to his honor, as "Clemency" Canning. At a banquet given the latter in London just before he sailed, he uttered these prophetic words: "I wish for a peaceful term of office. But I cannot forget that in the sky of India, serene as it is, a small cloud may arise, no larger than a man's hand, but which, growing larger and larger, may at last threaten to burst and overwhelm us with ruin."

The Sepoy Mutiny

Within the year the great mutiny of the Sepoys, in which Mohammedan and Hindu alike engaged, occurred, and the whole Ganges valley rose in rebellion against the English. The thrilling story of this awful rebellion, occurring precisely a century after the battle of Plassey, and nearly contemporaneously with our own War of Secession, cannot be recounted here. It began at Meerut, May 10, 1857, and a summer of horrors followed. It centred around the cities of Cawnpore, Lucknow, and Delhi, and its most dramatic scenes, famous in song and story, are connected with the heroism of John Nicholson, Havelock and his "Saints," the Fall of Delhi, the Relief of Lucknow after eighty-five days of siege, and Jessie Brown's never-to-be-forgotten cry, "Dinna ye hear the slogan?" The civilized world still shudders at "the awful silence of Cawnpore," when, after eleven days of hard fighting, Havelock entered the city and found not one of his countrymen left to receive him. Two days earlier, July 15, every English man, woman, and child, nine hundred in all, had been slaughtered, and two hundred of them hurled, whether dead or still alive, into a well. The war which followed this awful opening dragged on for many months longer, before the Mutiny was wholly quelled. To-day, in Cawnpore, a garden of roses blooms on the spot where that awful house of death stood, and over the covered well stands in white marble the form of the angel of peace.

Causes of the Mutiny

Precisely what led to the great Mutiny will perhaps never be determined. Wise men differ. Said Lord Lawrence, "I believe that what more tended to stir up the Indian Mutiny than any one thing was the habitual cowardice of Great Britain as to her own religion." Others attributed it to the inherent disparity between the white man and the Oriental, which causes an inevitable distrust. Deep below the surface, doubtless, was the smouldering, inevitable resentment of the conquered toward the conquerors, and the inborn dread of denationalization. On the surface was the alarm caused in the native mind by the rapid multiplication of telegraph wires and steam engines, and other tokens of a foreign civilization. Last of all, as the fuse which fires the mine, was a rumor running like wildfire through the Bengal army that the cartridges of a new set dealt out to them were greased with the fat of cows, the animal sacred to the Hindu, and with the fat of swine, the animal unclean alike to Hindu and Mohammedan. Did not this mean that their most sacred scruples were to be trampled upon? their caste broken?

Perhaps, as we read the story of the Sepoy Rebellion, we find it less surprising that such an event happened once than that it has not happened many times, with a population of two hundred and eighty-seven millions, and a standing army of but two hundred and thirty thousand, more than two-thirds of which are composed of natives.

Consequences of the Mutiny

The Mutiny led to the dissolution of the East India Company and the transfer of the administration of Indian affairs to the British crown.

On November 1, 1858, at a great *darbar* (court reception) held at Allahabad, Lord Canning gave the Royal Proclamation, which announced that the Queen of England had herself assumed the government of India. Nineteen years later, in January, 1877, with all the scenic effect of Oriental display and theatrical magnificence, at the ancient Mughal capital, Delhi, Queen Victoria was proclaimed Empress of India.

Thus has culminated the latest invasion of India, begun in 1600 for commerce, continued for conquest, resulting, let us hope, in the twentieth century in a stable, enlightened, and Christian commonwealth for the conquered people.

Character of British Rule

The British government has proceeded on the basis that it cannot introduce Christianity, but must rely on secular education and the arts and industries of the western world for the regeneration of the Indian peoples, thus seeking to form a new nation with a Christian civilization built up on a heathen foundation. The annual grants of the East India Company to heathen temples in some cases are still continued under government guarantee. To many thoughtful minds Great Britain is trying a dangerous experiment — a policy freighted with peril; a system, one has said, which "carries with it its own nemesis."

The character of British rule in India has,

however, been ennobled by the names of many enlightened Christian statesmen from the days of Lord Bentinck down to the present time. Lord Dalhousie, although forced by the exigencies of the time (1848–1856) to embark on a policy of annexation and to enter on wars with the Sikhs and the Burmese, was a high-minded statesman, a man of sensitive conscience, and a lover of peace. His deepest interest lay in the advancement of the moral and material welfare of India. No branch of administration escaped his reforming hand. Sir John Lawrence's name will be held in everlasting remembrance in the Punjab for his noble measures to relieve the famine sufferers in 1866–1869. He embodied what the natives of India most fear and most respect,—power, courage, kindness, and inexorable justice. He first laid down the principle that the officers of the government should be held personally responsible for taking every means to avoid death by starvation. Other illustrious names might be cited of those who kept steadily in view the theory that government was "for the good of the governed."

British India

As now constituted British India consists of the following twelve provinces: Bengal, Assam, Ajmere, North West Provinces, Oudh, Punjab, Central Provinces, Berar, Bombay, Coorg, Burma, Madras. Besides these which are directly under British rule there are several hundred "feudatory states" which are ruled *under British government* by their own hereditary princes. Of these the largest are Haidarabad, better known as "the Nizam's Dominions," and Rajputana, each with a population of nearly twelve millions.

The government of the Indian Empire is primarily in the hands of a secretary of state, but it is administered by a governor-general, or, as he is now more commonly called, a viceroy, appointed by the British crown and assisted by a council or cabinet of six members. The usual term of office for the viceroy and his cabinet is five years.

The supreme government has its official seat in Calcutta; but early in April it is customary for the viceroy and his cabinet to remove to Simla, the famous resort in the spurs of the Himalayas, for the hot season, that is, until late autumn.

Under the viceroy are governors, as of Madras, Calcutta, and Bombay; lieutenant-governors, as of Burma, Bengal, and the Punjab, and another class of subordinate rulers called chief commissioners, as of Assam. Below these are a large number of collectors, deputies, magistrates, and minor administrative officials. The unit of administration is the *District*, the whole number of which in British India is about 240, varying greatly in size and in number of inhabitants. The average area of a district is 3778 square miles; the average population 802,927 souls. Civil law is administered with marked justice. The final appeal is to the privy council of England. The district officer is "the backbone of administrative India."

The total population of British India by the latest census is 288,000,000.

The present viceroy is Lord Curzon, whose term began in 1899. Lady Curzon is an American woman, formerly Miss Mary Leiter of Chicago.

To sum up in the sententious language of Robert E. Speer: "India was not a nation. Therefore Great Britain conquered it and has held it. Great Britain is making it a nation. What will be the result?"

ILLUSTRATIVE SELECTIONS

Passage from the Proclamation of the Queen of England, July, 1858. Sometimes called the "Magna Charta of Indian Liberties."

We hold ourselves bound to the natives of our Indian territories by the same obligations of duty which bind us to all other subjects; and those obligations, by the blessing of Almighty God, we shall faithfully and conscientiously fulfil. Firmly relying ourselves on the truth of Christianity, and acknowledging with gratitude the solace of religion, we disclaim alike the right and the desire to impose our convictions on any of our subjects. We declare it to be our royal will and pleasure that none be in any wise favored, none molested or disquieted, by reason of their religious faith or observances; but that all shall alike enjoy the equal and impartial protection of the law; and we do strictly charge and enjoin all those who may be in authority under us, that they abstain from all interference with the religious belief or worship of any of our subjects, on pain of our highest displeasure.

Of the Mutiny it is truly said that it divides all Anglo-Indian history into two parts. Understand the Mutiny, and you understand India. . . . The East India Company had been sowing the wind; it was now to reap the whirlwind. It had leagued itself with idolatry; out of this unholy alliance came its death.

—Edward A. Lawrence.

Flashlights on the Country

If one could look down upon India from a balloon, one would see that it was more or less divided into three regions. The first is the Himalayas, the second is the plains of Hindustan, the third is the Deccan, a great three-sided tableland which covers the southern half of India. It slopes upward from the plains, and its northern wall and buttresses (the Vindhya Mountains) stood in former times as a vast barrier of mountain and jungle between northern and southern India, greatly increasing the difficulty of welding the whole into one empire, until at length pierced by road and rail. The eastern and western sides of the Deccan are known as Ghats. In the Bombay presidency the Ghats rise in magnificent precipices and headlands almost out of the ocean, and truly look like colossal landing stairs from the sea. The eastern and western Ghats meet at an angle near Cape Comorin at the southern extremity, and so complete the sides of the tableland.—ISABEL SAVORY.

The front door of India, Bombay, is magnificent; the back door, the Khyber Pass, is shabby. Out of the rose hedges of Peshawar a dust-yellow road carries you through a dust-gray plain, heading for dust-drab mountains. India seems worn out, giving up the weary effort to be soil, reverting limply to rock, sand, mud.

A new India—the Deccan. Uneven, colorless tableland, undecided shapes of colorless mountains, gemmed here and there with dazzling green and scarlet—that is the type of the whole vast triangle.

Haidarabad—not so much a city as a masque of mediæval Asia. Everywhere I breathed Islam and the Middle Ages. Think of the sheer joy of riding on an elephant through the streets of a city where they still maintain a royal regiment of Amazons.

—G. W. STEEVENS.

The white dust in the highways and the stenches in the byways are a very present evil; with the flies, mosquitoes, weary heat, and endless glare, they swell the items in the long bill which the white man pays for serving his grim stepmother country.—ISABEL SAVORY.

Bombay is half Oriental, half Occidental. It has the rush of Chicago, the fashion of Paris, and the cosmopolitanism of London. — H. C. MABIE.

Stand on the Hughli bridge at Calcutta at sunset, on the east side the factory smoke lying in a sullen bank under the glowing scarlet; on the west, the corn-field of masts, and the funnel smoke and the city smoke fouling the ineffable stillness of Indian evening, and the Bengalis crossing the bridge. On one side going into Calcutta, on the other coming out, an endless drove of moving, white-clothed people, never varying in thickness, never varying in pace, never stopping, no interval, just moving, moving like an endless belt running on a wheel. Just population — that is Bengal.

Madras! At last here is the India that was expected — the India of our childhood and of our dreams. The air is moist, the sky intensely blue. You drive on broad roads of red sand, through colonnades of red-berried banyans and thick groves of dipping palms, by pools and streams of soft green water. And the people are just as you have always seen them in your mind — naked above the loins, petticoated below, any color from ochre to umber . . . lithe little coolies in loin-cloths, they pass by in a perpetual panorama of popular India — the India you knew before you came. I am convinced that Little Henry's Bearer was a Madrasi.

India is amazing and stupefying at the first glance, and amazing and stupefying it remains to the last. . . . It strikes you as very, very old — burned out, sapless, tired. Its people for the most part are small, languid, effeminate. . . . Everywhere the same grotesque contradictions — splendor and squalor, divinity and dirt, superstition and manliness. The western mind can make nothing of it, cannot bring it into focus. You simply hold your head, and say that this is the East, and you are of the West.

And the Himalayas and the eternal snows? Up and up I toiled. Then at a sudden turn of the winding ascent I saw the summit of Kinchinjunga — just the summit, poised in the blue, shining and rejoicing in the sunrise. And as I climbed, other peaks rose into sight below and beside him, all dazzling white, mounting and mounting the higher I mounted, every instant more huge and towering and stately, boring the sky. . . . It was not a range, but a country of mountains. . . . It was the end of the world — a sheer rampart, which forbade the fancy of anything beyond. — G. W. Steevens.

Go to India. The Taj alone is worth the journey.
— Lord Roberts.

What the People Said

(June 21, 1887)

By the well where the bullocks go,
Silent and blind and slow,
By the field where the young corn dies,
In the face of the sultry skies,
They have heard, as the dull earth hears,
The voice of the wind of an hour,
The sound of the great Queen's voice: —
"My God hath given me years,
Hath granted dominion and power;
And I bid you, O land, rejoice."

And the ploughman settles the share
More deep in the grudging clod;
For he saith: "The wheat is my care,
And the rest is the will of God.

He sent the Mahratta spear
As He sendeth the rain,
And the *Mlech*, in the fated year,
Broke the spear in twain,
And was broken in turn. Who knows
How our lords make strife?
It is good that the young wheat grows,
For the bread is life."

Then, far and near, as the twilight drew,
Hissed up to the scornful dark
Great serpents, blazing, of red and blue,
That rose and faded, and rose anew,
That the land might wonder and mark.
"To-day is a day of days," they said;
"Make merry, O people, all!"
And the ploughman listened and bowed his head:—
"To-day and to-morrow God's will," he said,
As he trimmed the lamps on the wall.

"He sendeth us years that are good,
As He sendeth the dearth.
He giveth to each man his food,
Or her food to the earth.
Our kings and our queens are afar,—
On their peoples be peace,—
God bringeth the rain to the Bar,
That our cattle increase."

And the ploughman settles the share
More deep in the sun-dried clod,—
"Mogul, Mahratta, and *Mlech* from the north,
And White Queen over the seas—
God raiseth them up and driveth them forth
As the dust of the ploughshare flies in the breeze;
But the wheat and the cattle are all my care,
And the rest is the will of God."

— RUDYARD KIPLING.

The white invasion has done India good just in measure as it has been accompanied by genuine, religious influence. So far as it has been commercial and indifferent merely, it has done harm. England has unselfishly done for India more, I think, than any other nation would do, but she has failed to give her an upward impulse. . . . The only salvation of India, even from an economic point of view, in the opinion of those who have longest and most deeply studied it, is its Christianization. Let England inspire India with a veritable Christian faith, and nine-tenths of the present difficulties would spontaneously cease.—JULIAN HAWTHORNE.

THE BASIS OF BRITISH EMPIRE

If the feeling of a common nationality began to exist in India only feebly—if, without inspiring any active desire to drive out the foreigner, it only created a notion that it was shameful to assist him in maintaining his dominion—from that day, almost, our empire would cease to exist; for of the army by which it is garrisoned, two-thirds consist of native soldiers. . . . So long as the population has not formed the habit of criticising their government, whatever it may be, and rebelling against it, the government of India from England is possible. . . . On the other hand, if this feeling ever does spring up; if India does begin to breathe as a national whole,—and our own rule is perhaps doing more than ever was done by former governments to make this possible,—then the feeling would soon gain the native army, and on the native army we ultimately depend. . . . The moment a mutiny is threatened which shall be no mere mutiny, but the expression of a universal feeling of nationality, at that moment all hope is at an end, as all desire ought to be at an end, of preserving our empire. For we are not really conquerors of India, and we cannot rule her as conquerors; if we undertook to do so . . . we should assuredly be ruined financially by the mere attempt.

— Professor Seeley, in *The Expansion of England.*

Prayer from the Koran

In the name of God, the compassionate Compassioner. Praise be to God, the Lord of the worlds, the compassionate Compassioner, the Sovereign of the day of judgment. Thee do we worship and of Thee do we beg assistance. Direct us in the right way; in the way of those to whom Thou hast been gracious, on whom there is no wrath, and who go not astray.

Jesus Christ, according to the Koran, is only one of six apostles specially chosen to proclaim new dispensations in confirmation of previous ones. These are Adam, Noah, Abraham, Moses, Jesus, and Mohammed. The Koran makes the following declaration: "The Christians say Christ is the Son of God. May God resist them . . . how are they infatuated! . . ."

The creation of the race is described as follows: "Allah took into his hands a mass of clay, and, dividing it in two equal portions, he threw one-half into hell, saying, 'These to eternal fire, and I care not!' and, tossing the other upward, he added, 'These to paradise, and I care not!'"

Whatever good betideth thee is from God, and whatever betideth thee of evil is from thyself. — *Koran.*

God! there is no god but he, the living, the eternal. Slumber doth not overtake him, neither sleep; to him belongeth all that is in heaven and in earth. Who is he that can intercede with him but by his own permission?

He knoweth that which is past and that which is to come unto them, and they shall not comprehend anything of his knowledge but so far as he pleaseth. His throne is extended over heaven and earth, and the upholding of both is no burden unto him. He is the lofty and great.

(These sentences from the Koran are still often engraved on precious stones and worn by devout Mussulmans.)

"The Last Word of Islam to Europe"

in the year 1902 by the mouth of Sheik Abdul Hagk, of Bagdad: —

For us in the world there are only believers and unbelievers; love, charity, fraternity toward believers; contempt, disgust, hatred, and war against unbelievers. Amongst unbelievers the most hateful and criminal are those who, while recognizing God, attribute to Him earthly relationships, give Him a son, a mother. Learn then, European observers, that a Christian of no matter what position, from the simple fact that he is a Christian, is in our eyes a blind man fallen from all human dignity. Other infidels have rarely been aggressive toward us. But Christians have in all times shown themselves our bitterest enemies. . . . The only excuse you offer is that you reproach us with being rebellious against your civilization. Yes, rebellious, and rebellious till death! But it is you, and you alone, who are the cause of this. Great God! are we blind enough not to see the prodigies of your progress? But know, Christian conquerors, that no calculation, no treasure, no miracle can ever reconcile us to your impious rule. Know that the mere sight of your flag here is torture to Islam's soul; your greatest benefits are so many spots sullying our conscience, and our most ardent aspiration and hope is to reach the happy day when we can efface the last vestiges of your accursed empire.

"The Bengal Tiger"

"What would be the result if the British forces were to withdraw to-morrow from India?" recently asked a well-known American traveller of a Hindu high in rank. "What would be the result," was the answer, "if the bars were suddenly removed from all the cages in a menagerie? There would be a terrific fight all around among the wild beasts, and the wild beast that would come out ahead would be the Bengal tiger; and the Bengal tiger would be the Mohammedan."

Epitaph of Jehanara, the Mughal Cordelia

"Let no canopy cover my grave. This grass is the best covering for the poor in spirit. The humble, the transitory Jehanara, the disciple of the holy men of Christ, the daughter of the Emperor, Shah Jehan."

Selections from the Zend-Avesta

All good do I accept at thy command, O God, and think, speak, and do it. I believe in the pure law; by every good work seek I forgiveness for all sins. I keep pure for myself the serviceable work and abstinence from the unprofitable. I keep pure the six powers, — thought, speech, work, memory, mind, and understanding. According to thy will am I able to accomplish, O accomplisher of good, thy honor, with good thoughts, good words, good wishes.

I enter on the shining way to paradise; may the fearful terror of hell not overcome me! May I step over the bridge Chinevat, may I attain paradise, with much perfume and all enjoyments and all brightness.

Take up the white man's burden,
  Send forth the best ye breed,
Go, bind your sons to exile
  To serve your captives' need;
To wait, in heavy harness,
  On fluttered folk and wild,
Your new-caught, sullen peoples,
  Half devil and half child.

Take up the white man's burden —
  Ye dare not stoop to less —
Nor call too loud on Freedom
  To cloke your weariness.
By all ye will or whisper,
  By all ye leave or do,
The silent, sullen peoples
  Shall weigh your God and you."

— Rudyard Kipling.

From Edict VI of Asoka

(Carved on a pillar at Delhi)

I pray with every variety of prayer for those who differ from me in creed, that they, following my proper example, may with me attain unto eternal salvation.

Inscription on a Mohammedan Mosque

This world is a bridge. Pass thou over it, but build not upon it. This world is one hour; give its minutes to thy prayers; for the rest is unseen.

THEMES FOR STUDY OR DISCUSSION

I. Comparison between Buddhism and Christianity (Asoka and Constantine).
II. The Parsis in India.
III. Islam, the Ideal and the Real.
IV. Good and Evil Results of the Mohammedan Conquest. Famous Men and Women.
V. Comparison between the Reigns of Akbar the Great and Elizabeth of England.
VI. Agra and the Taj Mahal; the Mughals as Builders.
VII. Delhi, the Rome of India.
VIII. Christian English Statesmen of India.
IX. Calcutta and Bombay, Cities of Recent Growth.
X. Lord Clive and Warren Hastings.
XI The Sikhs, Rajputs, and Mahrattas.
XII. The Sepoy Mutiny, Cawnpore and Lucknow. (Read Tennyson's "The Defence of Lucknow" and R. Lowell's "The Relief of Lucknow.")

BOOKS OF REFERENCE

General References as before

Sir E. Arnold's "India Revisited," VI, VII, IX.
Butler's "Land of the Veda," III, IV, VI, XI, XII.
Carlyle's "On Heroes: Mahomet," III.
Clarke's "Ten Great Religions," I, II, III.
Dods' "Mohammed, Buddha, and Christ," I, III.
Fergusson's "Indian Architecture," IV, VI, VII.
Frazer's "British India," IV, V, VIII, X, XI, XII.
Humphreys' "Gems of India," IV, VI.
Hurst's "Indika," II, IV, VI, VII, IX, XII.
Kellogg's "Light of Asia and Light of the World," I.
Kipling's "City of the Dreadful Night," IX.
The Koran, III.

Leonowens's "Life and Travel in India," II, IV, IX.
Living Papers Series, "Non-Christian Religions of the World," I, II, III.
McCarthy's "History of our Own Times," VIII, XII.
Macaulay's "Essays," X.
Reed's "Persian Literature," II, III.
Rousselet's "India and its Native Princes," IV, VI, VII, IX, XI.
Bosworth Smith's "Mohammed and the Mohammedans," III.
Steevens's "In India," II, VI, VII, VIII, XI.
Thoburn's "India and Malaysia," I, II, III, IV.
Wheeler's "Short History of India." For all but I.
Sir M. Williams's "Religious Thought and Life in India," XI.
Sir M. Williams's "Buddhism," I.

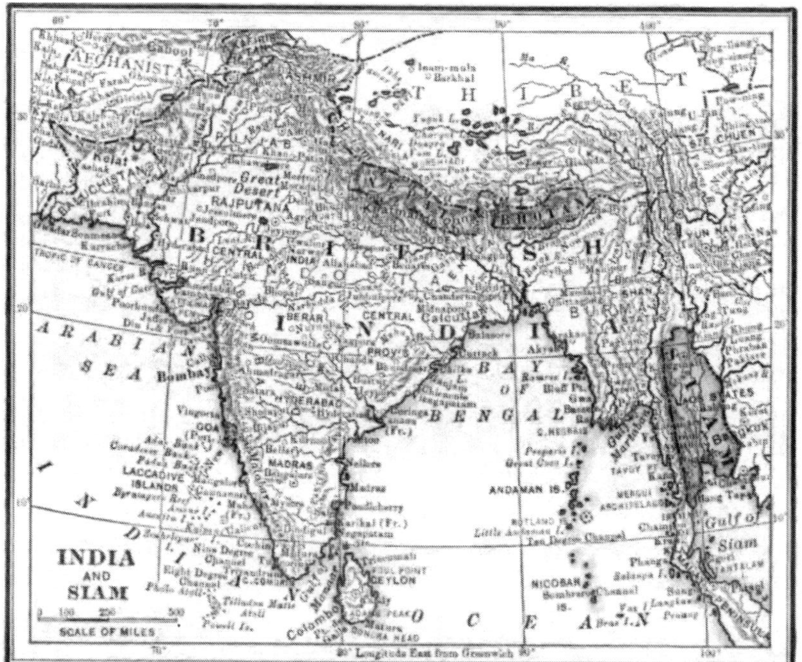
INDIA
AND
SIAM
SCALE OF MILES
AFGHANISTAN
BRITISH INDIA
THIBET
RAJPUTANA
Great Desert
CENTRAL INDIA
CENTRAL PROV'S
BERAR
HYDERABAD
MADRAS
Calcutta
Bombay
ARABIAN SEA
BAY OF BENGAL
INDIAN OCEAN
LACCADIVE ISLANDS
ANDAMAN IS.
NICOBAR IS.
CEYLON
Colombo
Gulf of Siam
Longitude East from Greenwich
RORMAY & CO., N.Y.

RELIGIOUS CENSUS, 1891[1]

Out of a thousand natives selected from the different religions in their due proportion, 723 would be Hindu, 199 Mohammedan, 24 Buddhist, 6 Sikh, 8 Christian, the remaining 40 pagans. The totals are as follows: —

Hindus		207,728,676
Mohammedan		57,321,164
Aboriginals		9,280,467
Buddhists (Burma) . . .		7,131,361
Christians (Prot.)	559,661	
" (other)	1,724,719	
		2,284,380[2]
Sikhs		1,907,833
Jains		1,416,638
Parsis		89,904
Jews		17,194
Brahmas		3,051
Miscellaneous		42,763
Total . . .		287,223,431

Languages

There are one hundred languages and fifty dialects spoken, due chiefly to the diversity of race. Every great invasion has been the signal for thrusting a new language upon the country. These languages may be divided into three groups, — the Aryan, Dravidian, Kolarian.

The original Aryan, from which all Indo-European tongues sprang, has perished. It developed into Sanskrit, the old classical language of government and higher education, now a dead language. The most important of the Aryan languages are: —

[1] For this table and those on the page following the author is indebted to the courtesy of the Foreign Missions Library.

[2] The census for 1901 shows an increase in this total of 638,969 for the decade.

Continued from page 85.

Language	Where Spoken	Population
Bengali	Lower Bengal	41,000,000
Uriya	Orissa	9,000,000
Assamese	Valley of Assam	1,500,000
Hindustani or Urdu and Hindi	N. W. Provinces, Rajputana, and Punjab	85,500,000
Marathi	Bombay and Deccan	18,750,000
Gujerati	Gugerat, commercial language throughout western India	10,500,000
Sindi	Sind	2,500,000
Punjabi	Punjab	17,750,000
Pushtu	British Afghanistan	1,000,000
Kashmiri	Valley of Kashmir	29,000

Of the Dravidian languages all but four are uncultivated, unwritten, and spoken only by uncivilized hill tribes. These four are:—

Language	Where Spoken	Population
Tamil	Madras to Cape Comorin (Ceylon)	15,000,000
Telugu	Lower basins of Kistna and Godavari	19,750,000
Kanarese	Mysore and northward	9,750,000
Malayalam	Travancore and Malabar coast	5,250,000

The Kolarian languages are all without character or literature, and are spoken only by hill tribes.

CHAPTER III

THE OFT-CONQUERED PEOPLE

Oh, masters, lords, and rulers in all lands,
How will the future reckon with this man?
How answer his brute question in that hour
When whirlwinds of rebellion shake the world?
How will it be with kingdoms and with kings,
With those who shaped him to the thing he is,
When this dumb terror shall reply to God
After the silence of the centuries?

—E. MARKHAM.

WHAT of the people themselves, so often conquered, so intermingled in strain?

It has been well said, there is no Indian people. There is a motley mass of humanity, of different races and tribes and a hundred tongues, composing the population of India, but they are no more a distinct nation than are the peoples of Europe.

The Hindus, however, Aryan and non-Aryan, have not been essentially amalgamated with their Mohammedan or British conquerors; their Brahmanical religion and the customs founded upon the Code of Manu remain substantially unchanged from ancient ages.

To the Hindu people, then, so greatly in excess of all others numerically in India, we must give our attention, with especial reference to the condition of women and the practices of religion.

I. STATUS AND CHARACTERISTICS OF THE HINDUS

About sixty per cent of the population of India [1] lives by agriculture. Ninety per cent is a rural population. In all India there are but twenty-eight cities numbering over 100,000 inhabitants, and but six whose populations exceed 200,000, viz., Bombay (821,764), Calcutta (741,144), Madras (452,518), Haidarabad (415,039), Lucknow (273,028), Benares (219,467).

The rural population, stolid and illiterate in the main, resides in villages; the common occupations beside agriculture are working as smiths, carpenters, oil-pressers, potters, and weavers. The houses, built of matting, wattles, or adobe, and roofed with reeds or grass, are primitive in structure and almost destitute of furnishing. The common life of the villagers is laborious, monotonous, and colorless to a degree. Rice, the staple article of food, is commonly cleansed and ground by the women.

There is little manufacture on a large scale, but in delicacy and beauty the silk and cotton fabrics, the embroidery, jewelry, and carpets of India are unexcelled in the world's products.

The Hindus are a civilized people, but their civilization seems to have remained stagnant for three thousand years. Life is on a dead level.

[1] Two hundred and eighty-eight millions total.

"It tires one," says a recent English traveller, "to see the fixedness, the apathy, the lifelessness of a great population which should by right be up and stirring, trading, and organizing. There is a strange mingling in the Oriental of impassiveness and childishness, of fierce passions and primitive ideas." Not inaptly have the Hindus been called "a nation of children."

Racial Characteristics

The physical characteristics of the leading races in India have been thus described by a French authority:—the *Aryan type* (chiefly represented in its purity by the Rajput and Brahman) is marked by a long head; the face is long, symmetrical, and narrow; the nose is straight and delicate; the forehead is well developed; features regular, and the facial angle high; in stature he is somewhat tall; the complexion is clear, and even fair in some cases.

The *Dravidian type* inclines somewhat toward the long head; the nose is large and broad; facial angle comparatively low; lips are thick; face large and fleshy; features coarse and irregular; height low; complexion varies from brown to almost black.

The *Mongol type* (including Tibeto-Burman and Kolarian) is marked by a short head; the face is large; nose short and large; the cheekbones are high and prominent; the eyes appear to be set awry upon the face.

While less muscular than the European, the Hindu is more graceful in his movements. The height, strength, and courage of those dwelling in the north are generally greater than are found in southern India. The average duration of life is twenty-four years, against nearly forty-four years in England.

The Hindus are docile, gentle, peaceable, and temperate, courteous to a degree, affectionate, and naturally religious. Of fair intelligence, and, in the Brahman caste, capable of a refinement of philosophic subtlety in thinking, they are singularly unresponsive to social and intellectual progress. Instead of creative or inventive energy, in the higher type of Hindu we have a dreamy, speculative, brooding habit of mind; instead of manly and cheerful courage, a fixed fatalism; instead of calm reason, a feverish and unwholesome imagination; in place of patriotism, among the poorer classes at least, a dull indifference as to who rules his land if only he be suffered to plough his field and eat his rice in peace. Throughout the nation there is, in place of the stern and rugged virtues of freemen, a passive subservience, a loss of the power of self-government, an absence of ambition in almost every field of activity. "We are a subject race," said Protap Chunder Mozoomdar; "we are uneducated; we are incapable."

A good illustration of the contrast between the progressive American and the conservative

Hindu is offered by the fact that while in the Patent Office in Washington there are models for six thousand improved ploughs, the inhabitants of India use the same implement which was used by their progenitors at least two thousand years ago.

The characteristics named are obviously those of a people so often conquered that the power of energetic action, the principles of patriotism and national integrity, have been almost crushed out, for the story of their past is but the long monotony of repeated conquest and oppression. "The White Queen over the Sea" has been to the people at large but a species of fabulous fairy allotted by Fate to rule over them for a time.

Poverty and Famine

The tropical, enervating climate, together with imperfect agricultural methods and frequent droughts, gives rise to a condition of extreme poverty in itself essentially productive of a low vitality and a physical languor almost fatal to the development of the spirit of personal and public progress. It must be also borne in mind that the density of the population of India, nearly eleven times greater to the square mile than that of the United States, contributes powerfully to conditions of poverty and suffering.

While the magnificent spectacle attending the proclamation of Queen Victoria as Empress of India was holding the eye of the world in the year 1877, the shadow of a famine more terrible than had been known in a century was darkening southern India. As a result of the conditions which followed, the deaths from starvation, and disease incident to lack of food, were estimated at five million two hundred and fifty thousand.

During the last quarter of a century, that is since the famine of 1876–1877, there have been sixteen great famines, resulting in over twenty million deaths, a startling increase over the record for any previous period of the same length.

The plague and famine of 1897, in northern central India, directly involved in indescribable sufferings a population of thirty-seven millions, while thrice that number were in the region of "scarcity."

Average Incomes

It is possible that to the English or American reader the ordinary conditions of life among the Hindus would appear to merit the term "scarcity," which is usually applied only to famine conditions. The official estimate of the average Indian income for those outside government positions in 1882 was three cents a day, or eleven dollars a year for each person. In 1900 it has been estimated as a cent and a half a day. These figures will indicate the profound and increasing poverty of the people at large. It may also lead thoughtful readers to wonder less at the apathy, the fatalism, the spiritless and stoical lethargy of the nation.

The average yearly salary of India's native officials in the British civil and military service for the year 1898–1899 was one hundred and eighty dollars. The average salary of her English officials, who of necessity occupy the more responsible positions, was three thousand dollars for the same year. In official position the Englishman undoubtedly has the preference over the native, and in all the higher positions this preference practically amounts almost to monopoly. It is pardonable, then, as says Bishop Thoburn, if the Indian looks upon the English youth who comes out to take up work in India, as something more than a rival, as rather an unjust supplanter of the children of the soil.

A careful student of the financial condition of British India at the beginning of the twentieth century writes, "Nearly the whole of the wealth remaining in the country a hundred years ago has been so drained away that there is now less popular pecuniary reserve in India than in any civilized country in the world."

It has been estimated that forty millions of the people habitually live on one meal a day, and it is a matter of course for multitudes to lie down to sleep hungry every night. "A patient people, these villagers of India; they have been hungry these thirty centuries, and it has never occurred to them that they have any claim to be filled."

II. THE POSITION OF WOMEN IN THE HINDU ECONOMY

The wrongs of Indian womanhood have been frequently and movingly set forth.

Let us begin our study of this topic, however, by stating that though much is wrong, *all* is not wrong. The Hindus are better than Hinduism. Harsh and brutal as are the dicta of the Code of Manu on the subject of women, the inborn laws of humanity, the practical requirements of daily social and domestic life, and above all the power of natural affection, have greatly softened the application of those laws.

Woman in the Vedas

Even the Sanskrit books have some fine conceptions of womanly attributes, and the early Vedas held women in high regard. In later literature the ideal woman is described as a pattern of worldly and self-centred perfection: she is to keep all her husband's secrets, never to reveal the amount of his wealth, to excel all other women in personal attractiveness, in knowledge of cookery, in hospitality and in thrift, and in superintending every detail of family life. Finally, she is to coöperate with her husband in pursuing the three great objects of life,—religious *merit*, wealth, and enjoyment. This perfect woman is called a *Padmini* (a lotus flower of womankind). In short, the highest ideal of Hindu womanhood approximates closely the lowest standard of Christian womanhood, —falsely called Christian, since it names but knows not Christ.

Seclusion of Women

It is not probable that the early Hindus ever enforced the seclusion of their women. This practice is due to Mohammedan influences, and, in actual fact, concerns only a small percentage even of high-caste Hindu women. In the Mahratta country, in western India, and in many districts where Mohammedan influence has not prevailed, the women enjoy a large degree of freedom.

Those who are confined in the Zenana (a Mohammedan term) or behind the Purdah (the Hindu for veil or curtain) consider their lot a very exalted one and a token of their aristocratic superiority, although they may never have enjoyed a good ride or walk in their lives, or seen anything of the world outside their comfortless quarters. The women's apartments, even in elegant marble mansions in the great cities, are in the back of the house, gloomy and inferior, dull and prison-like. The native dress of the women consists of a small jacket and a *sari*, *i.e.* six to nine yards of cloth, one end of which is wrapped around the waist, gathered into folds in front, and secured by tucking under. When required, this end may be readily loosed and used as a head covering. If the husbands are wealthy, the women load themselves with the gorgeous, barbaric jewels of which all Indian women are so fond, and spend their time in vacant idleness or in elaborate, voluptuous baths and anointings. Otherwise, they have the resource of cookery and other domestic occupation. The sole subjects for conversation in the belittling life of the Zenana are the pettiest gossip, and the tedious intrigues of the complex household in which four generations may be included, with several wives and concubines for every man. Intellectual life, philanthropy, patriotic and public interests there are none. So deep is the prejudice against the movement for the education of women that the recent severe droughts have been ascribed to the displeasure of the gods on this account. It has been a popular belief among high-caste women that their husbands would die if they should even learn to read or write.

Common Characteristics

Notwithstanding these and many depressing influences, the ties of family life are strong in India, perhaps the most hopeful fact in the problem of uplifting the people. The mother of sons enjoys a species of honor and respect, and a mother-in-law rules her sons' wives with despotic authority. The married women, while held as servile inferiors to their husbands, are gentle, retiring, and not devoid of personal beauty; patience and tenderness are chief characteristics, and the love of children amounts in many cases to a passion; while, on the other hand, instances of most unnatural cruelty are not uncommon. In the gentler features of Hindu womanhood above mentioned dwell the promise and potency of a noble future for the race; but there are social conditions which stand like an almost insurmountable barrier between actual conditions and such a consummation. For women of moral and intellectual excellence are exceptions, and until Asiatic women, whether Hindu or Moslem, are elevated and educated, all efforts to raise Asiatic nations to the level of Anglo-Saxon will remain fruitless.

Of the average Hindu woman it can be truly said: her birth is unwelcome, her physical life is outraged, her mental life is stunted, her spiritual life is denied existence. Female infanticide, while no longer openly committed, is known to be still prevalent, especially among the Rajputs, who are too proud to make inferior alliances for their daughters, or too poor to provide several with the large dowry which extravagant custom has fixed, and therefore quietly put superfluous girl babies out of the way.

Family Life

The "joint-family system" of India is a dangerous one to family peace; jealousy and hatred, discord and deceit, rule. Family feuds and litigations are everyday occurrences. The Hindu family is an incoherent and cumbrous mass. Upon the children are concentrated the power of evil example and every aspect of domestic unhappiness. A sad feature of home life is the prurient precocity of children, who begin their vile language in their infant prattle, and grow old in pollution while young in years. "The child's life is full of misery. The indecent speech of the home is one of its darkest features. Worse than all is the woe of Indian childhood which befalls the opening mind when, led by their mothers to the Indian temple, their eyes are met with sights, their ears assailed with songs, of such loathsome import, that innocency may not sustain the strain, and the child mind perishes in that awful hour."

The average Indian mother never thinks of paying attention to the moral or mental development of her little children, while, as they usually go unclad and often unwashed, her cares for their physical life are simple. The lack of sanitary knowledge involves habits of life filthy beyond description.

Polygamy is not common among the lower

class of Hindus, although permitted to the Brahmans, and to all if the wife fails to bear a son after seven years. Among Mohammedans it is prevalent, while open concubinage is common to all classes in India. The widespread ignorance of Indian women is evidenced by statistics which show that in 1897 there were but six women out of every thousand who could read or write. If the women above twenty-five years of age are reckoned, we find that the percentage of illiterates is ninety-nine and one-half, indicating that female education is almost confined to this generation.

A Mohammedan Household

"In a rich man's harem," says Isabella Bishop, "there are women of all ages and colors, girl children, and very young boys. There are the favorite and other legitimate wives, concubines, who have recognized, but very slender, rights, discarded wives who have been favorites in their day, and who have passed into practical slavery to their successors, numbers of slaves and old women, daughters-in-law, and child or girl widows whose lot is deplorable, and many others. I have seen as many as two hundred in one house, a great crowd, privacy being unknown, grossly ignorant, with intolerable curiosity forcing on a stranger abominable or frivolous questions, then relapsing into apathy but rarely broken, except by outbreaks of hate and the results of successful intrigue." The Moslem population remains a sullen and ominous element in the life of India. The youths are proverbially slow to acquire education. The men and women are in no way superior in intelligence, morality, or industry to the Hindus.

Child Marriage

At the foundation of all the wrongs to Indian womanhood lies the practice of enforced child-marriage, with its concomitant of child-widowhood.

The custom of child-marriage is at least five hundred years older than the Christian era, and doubtless sprang from the belief that a man had no claim to the funeral ceremonial rites of his religion unless he was the father of a son, and that for an unmarried woman there was no salvation.

Little girls are betrothed in their cradles, or at the age of three or four, to boys a little older, of whom they know nothing, until, at the age of seven or eight, and from that up to twelve as the maximum, they are claimed as wives, and conducted to the homes of their husbands.

Motherhood at the age of ten or twelve is not infrequent, and many grandmothers are but twenty-five. Thus Hindu custom ordains that the women of India shall bear children while they are still children themselves, and a stunted, degenerate, and ill-developed race is the inevitable result.

"It must be borne in mind," says Ramabai, "that both in northern and southern India the term 'marriage' in infancy does not mean anything more than an irrevocable betrothal. The ceremony gone through at that time establishes religiously the conjugal relationship of both parties; there is a second ceremony which confirms the relationship both religiously and socially, which does not take place until the children attain the age of puberty." The Hindu people, as we now see, are not merely a "nation of children" but of the children of children. Marriage contracted and children born when there is no adequate means of support is furthermore a productive cause of the grinding poverty of the country. Hindu Swamis boast that there is no divorce in India. No, for marriage — unconsciously contracted child-marriage — is irrevocable for the wife, while the husband has no need of divorce, since he can desert his wife if he choose, and can install other women in his household if so minded.

Child Widows

Child-marriage entails the yet more awful system of child-widowhood, so blasting to all which makes life worth living that it has been termed "cold suttee," and many persons have felt that the ancient and now forbidden practice of widow-burning, by which the widow passed by death from the long martyrdom of life now her portion, was almost preferable.

Sir William Hunter quotes the following, which we will give as a typical case of child-widowhood: "Let us take the instance of a child of three years. This is not an exceptional but a fairly general instance. Of the fact that she has been once married and has become a widow she knows nothing. She, therefore, mixes with children not widowed. Supposing there is a festivity, children run to the scene; but the sight of a widowed child is a bad omen to the persons concerned in the festivities. She is removed by force. She cries, and is rewarded by her parents with a blow accompanied by remarks such as these: 'You were a most sinful being in your previous births, you have, therefore, been widowed already. Instead of hiding your shame in a corner of the house, you go and injure others.' . . . The child can wear no ornaments. She cannot bathe in the manner that other children bathe. Her touch is pollution. In the meanwhile, if the priest happens to visit the place where the child is, her head is immediately shaved and she is dressed in the single, coarse garment of the widow. She is then asked to eat only once in the day, and required to fast once a fortnight, even at the risk of death, the fast sometimes continuing for seventy-two hours."

The name "rand," by which the widow is generally known, is equivalent to the term "harlot." Ill treated by her family, or the family of her dead husband, in which she may dwell, as a contemptible, disgraceful being, it is no wonder that the young widow often seeks escape. But whither can she go? No respectable family will have her for a servant. She has been rendered repulsive in appearance by the shaving of her head; she is absolutely ignorant, absolutely destitute, owning only her single garment. The alternatives before her are submission to her wretched lot, suicide, or a life of infamy. Suicide is common; still more common the life of shame. It is largely from the class of child-widows that the ranks of the temple girls are recruited.

Religious Prostitution of Womanhood

The social and religious system of Hinduism brings in its train the dishonoring of women in a degree little understood by the western world.

The service of the temples demands large numbers of dancing-girls, or priestesses, who are dedicated in infancy to this vocation. When arrived at womanhood, they give their bodies to the service and maintenance of the temple, and form one of the most fruitful sources of the depravity of the Brahman priesthood, to whose pleasure they are primarily devoted. These temple girls are called *devadasis*, meaning slaves of the god.

Another class of courtesans, more familiar to European travellers in India, are the nautch girls.

The institution of the nautch is a very ancient one, based upon the example of the god Krishna, who sported with thousands of dancing-girls. Hence social custom sanctions their presence at all weddings, receptions, and functions of every kind. The nautch girl, being the only woman in India, until recent times, who had intellectual life or training, or any freedom in society, has held a somewhat honored place, corresponding in a way to the professional courtesan in the old Greek social fabric. All other women in India are strictly forbidden to dance, and education in a girl is still regarded in conservative Indian circles as a mark of loose morality.

The nautch girl is taught from earliest childhood to read, dance, and sing, and instructed in every art of seduction. These girls are usually beautiful and graceful, and they follow their profession with the characteristic submission of all Hindu women. They frequently acquire large fortunes, receiving extravagant gifts from wealthy Brahmans who come under the fascination of their wit, beauty, and accomplishments.

The muralis are girls devoted by their parents in infancy to the god Khandoba, a deity of the Maratha country. The rites of this dedication are termed "being married to a sword," the weapon of Khandoba. These muralis are licensed by law and dedicated to impure lives in the name of their religion. If you ask what can justify such action on the part of the parents, you will be told by the natives, "It is our custom." Custom in India is indeed religion.

III. THE PRACTICES OF THE HINDU RELIGION

In certain theoretical points Hinduism possesses affinities for Christianity, and the Hindu is more accessible than the Mussulman to Christian motives. Hinduism is a theistic religion; it upholds belief in a trinity, in divine self-revelation and incarnation; it inculcates the deepest reverence for and submission to God. The Hindus are a naturally religious people; and the resignation and patience which so peculiarly characterize them, with the exception of the Brahman caste, predispose them to the reception of the meek and lowly Redeemer. So much on the theoretical side.

We must now look at the practical working of the system in the common life of the people. It is not a congenial task to point out the weakness and failure of religious conceptions which are accepted by nearly one-fifth of the human race. It would be far more agreeable at this point to seek to discover something pure and helpful in the practices of Brahmanism, if this were honestly possible. The curse of India is, that its gods are the base productions of the polluted imaginations of its people.

Apologists for Hinduism

Great in the past has been the restraint of missionaries and travellers. Too great, perhaps, in view of the glamour which certain champions of Hinduism have of late striven to throw over it. As if by tacit consent, the darker features of Hindu worship have been left shrouded in silence and mystery, as being too repulsive to mention. It has been reserved, however, until these later days for civilized and Christianized men and women to dream of apologizing for idolatry and the nameless rites of Hindu shrines. But the time has now come when idolatry is not only apologized for as an innocent aid to devotion, but the system of which it is the concrete expression is idealized, when it is even held up, and not in vain, for the admiration of the Christian world. These tendencies are leading to a distinctly felt reaction and to a crisis in the history of missionary endeavor which a generation ago no one could have foreseen.

It must be borne in mind that the apologists for Brahmanism who have gained influence in England and America, even though they be Brahman priests have been trained in English schools and shaped by English environment, until they have learned how to present their system in a form artfully idealized to suit the western mind, and stripped for the time being of all repulsive features.

Idolatry

However subtle their pantheism in theory, in practice the Hindus are grossly idolatrous. Straightforward Hindu testimony utterly disproves the fine-spun theories of Brahman apologists. Over and over do the heathen themselves testify that the material form of the idol fills the mind and unfits it for any spiritual conception. "Idolatry is the curse of Hindustan," says Keshub Chunder Sen, "the deadly canker which has eaten into the vitals of native society."

The famous Rajah Rammohun Roy says: "I have observed that both in their writings and conversation many Europeans feel a wish to palliate and soften the features of Hindu idolatry, and are inclined to inculcate the idea that all objects of worship are considered by their votaries as emblematical representatives of the Supreme Divinity. *The truth is, the Hindus of the present day have no such view of it.* Neither do the Hindus regard the images of their gods merely in the light of instruments for elevating the mind to the conception of those supposed beings; *they are simply in themselves made objects of worship.*"

It is well to put this statement of a learned Hindu beside the futile benevolence of Sir Edwin

Arnold, who describes the Brahman priests in the temples at Benares giving him "flower wreaths from the necks of their idols and *smiling assent* when I said that no 'Twice-born' who had read his Bhagavad-Gita could believe in stone Mahadeos (Sivas) and wooden Guṇpatis (Ganesas) except as symbols."

Truly if all that is wanted in defence of Hinduism is a "smile of assent" in response to a leading question, the defence may not be lacking.

The Singer of the "Light of Asia," who is certainly not biassed by anti-Hindu prejudice, further tells us that while "Sakya-Muni's teaching did away with the bloody rites of the Brahmanic period, there are still immolations of a sad kind practised secretly in India. The Bheels and Chamars cast themselves occasionally from lofty rocks near Jairad, hoping to be Rajahs in the next state of life. In 1877 a Gosain of Benares sacrificed a boy of twelve in order to discover treasure. In 1883 a Banya family of twelve persons committed suicide in unison to 'please the gods,'" etc. Indifference to suffering and to human life are deeply ingrained in the dispositions of the people, less from cruelty than from fatalistic apathy.

Animal and Plant Worship

Again Sir Edwin Arnold exclaims: "One cannot be a day in this land without observing how the ancient *worship of the cow still holds the minds of the Hindus*. . . . Good Brahmans will feed a cow before they take their own breakfast, exclaiming, 'Daughter of Surabhi, formed of five elements, auspicious, pure, and holy, sprung from the sun, accept this food from me. Salutation and peace!' Everything which comes from the cow is sacred and purifying,—the droppings are plastered with water over the floors and verandas of all native houses and upon the cooking places; the ashes of the same commodity are used with coloring powders to mark the foreheads, necks, and arms of the pious," etc.

So efficiently hallowing is the cow in popular esteem that the serious pollution of a visit to England may be done away by the penance of Santapana, *i.e.* by swallowing a pill composed of the five products of the sacred beast. There is a famous Hindu saying, "There are many sects in India, but upon two main points we all agree,—the sanctity of the cow and the depravity of women."

The bull ranks next to the cow, and the worship of snakes and monkeys is universally prevalent. Hanuman, the black-faced monkey-god, is the especial guardian of Mahratta villages.

Witchcraft and demoniacal possession enter essentially into the common consideration of the people, whose superstition is wellnigh incredible, and who are at the mercy of the most appalling and sickening fears.

The fish, the tortoise, and the bear are worshipped as incarnations of Vishnu. The shrub called tulasi, or holy basil, is regarded as divine, and is *par excellence* a woman's deity. The pipal tree is supposed to be a residence of the god Brahma, and is sometimes invested with the sacred thread, all the ceremonies of investiture being performed over it. The bilva tree, with its triple leaf, is sacred to Siva, and its leaves are continually placed on the ling and on the bull.

Water Worship

Running water is everywhere held to be "instinct with deity." The famous Ganges ("Mother Gunga") is the holiest river of India. "No sin is too heinous to be removed, no character too black to be washed clean by its waters." Countless temples line its banks; countless priests stand ready to aid the worshippers in their ablutions. The conflux of the Jumna and the Ganges is the very holy of holies to the Hindu. Bottles of Ganges water are sent to all parts of the country, and have been used by local justices in administering oaths side by side with the Christian Bible and the Koran. The Narbada River is also counted peculiarly sacred. Death on the banks of either of these rivers is ardently desired by every orthodox Hindu.

Goddess Worship

Yet lower than all forms of nature worship is that of the female principle, or goddess worship, of which Monier Williams, the famous Sanskrit scholar, writes as follows: "It might have been expected that a creed which admits of an infinite multiplication of female deities would be likely to degenerate into various forms of licentiousness on the one hand and of witchcraft on the other. In Saktism we are indeed confronted with the worst results of the worst superstitious ideas that have ever disgraced and degraded the human race. It is by offering to women the so-called homage of sensual love and carnal passion, and by yielding free course to all the grosser appetites, wholly regardless of social rules and restrictions, that the worshippers of the female power (Sakti) in nature seek to gratify the goddess. Incredible as it may appear, these so-called worshippers actually affect to pride themselves on their debasing doctrines, because to indulge the grosser appetites and passions, with the mind fixed on union with the Supreme Being, is believed to be the highest of all pious achievements."

These detestable rites of Saktism are known as the "left-hand" method of worship, and the initiated call themselves "the perfect ones."

Distorted Conceptions

"These are our gods!" cry the Hindus complacently, as they point to the monkey-faced Hanuman, the elephant-headed Ganesa, the unspeakable Linga, the shapeless Mata Devi, the bloodthirsty Kali, the licentious Krishna, and many millions more. No religion known to humanity possesses a subtler mysticism, combined with a more manifold or more brutal pollution, than does Hinduism. "The grave Brahman will unreel you systems of metaphysics compared with which the 'Critique of Pure Reason' is simple and concrete; then he will depart and make his offering to a three-headed goddess covered with grease and red paint."

Undoubtedly the popular Krishna has done more for the debauchery of Hindu youth than any other god or demigod. He was the eighth great avatar of Vishnu, and his cult is one of the most modern as well as most universal of the Hindu system. His jovial democratic nature and limitless amours seem to endear him peculiarly to the mind of the lower classes. The story of his life and the details of his worship are unfit to print or read.

Brindaban, the unholy city, famed as the birthplace of Krishna, is the seat of one thousand temples to this most popular deity. Hundreds of thousands of Hindus make pilgrimage to it every year. It is one of the vilest cities on earth. Six thousand girls, mostly child-widows, serve as temple prostitutes in the Krishna service. The devotees on the occasions of these, as of most of the great festivals, give themselves up to the vilest orgies, equal in grovelling sensuality to those of the ancient Baal and Ashtaroth worship. Heathenism remains now as of old a filthy abomination.

A very curious coalition of Brahman and Buddhistic doctrines is found in the Vaishnava worship of Jagan-nath, literally "the Lord of the World." The apostle of this cult was Caitanya, a contemporary of Luther, who lived for many years at Pouri in Orissa, in close proximity to the temple of this most uncouth of deities. The triple image of Jagan-nath represents without doubt the Brahman *Tri-murti*, whereas his car festival is a reproduction of the Tooth Festival of the Buddhists. The most significant features of this festival, furthermore, the temporary abolition of caste and the worship of relics (Krishna's bones are supposed to repose inside the image), are essentially non-Brahman and Buddhistic. The former suicide of Brahman fanatics, by throwing themselves under the wheels of the car of Jagan-nath, is now forcibly prevented by mounted policemen, who guard the annual processions.

It is impossible to pass over in silence the thirty millions of *Linga* scattered everywhere through India, as the Mohammedans found them in the seventh century, by the roadside, on temple walls, and on idol chariots. This phallic emblem is the symbol of Siva, the regenerator, and is thought by some theorists and scholars to be wholly mystical in meaning, and not to involve sensual ideas. To those who have lived long, however, in India, and have observed the intimate working of Linga worship, it is plainly seen to be the source of much of the impurity of life and corruption of morals. A certain small temple at Benares, with its spire overlaid with gold, contains a stone lingam so sacred that to have performed acts of worship before it once in one's lifetime insures entry to the Brahmanic paradise. This revolting symbol is the focus of the great annual pilgrimage to Benares. Here the eager worshippers throng by the thousand, prostrating themselves before the emblem and drinking from the "holy well" of Siva, hard by, draughts of fetid, greenish water.

Said a well-known lecturer on India, writing on the spot in 1881: "India is so much worse than any one can describe it; the people are so much more vile than can be imagined; the forms of vice are all so disgusting! If you will consider that for generations every power that wicked imaginations can devise has been used to develop the lowest passions of both men and women, when the most widely worshipped god is the mere personification of the most debasing of sins, you can imagine the condition of things."

We have purposely drawn the statements given above from sources almost wholly secular, non-partisan, and non-missionary. They are the undeniable facts of common observation familiar to all residents in India and students of Hinduism.

Religion divorced from Morality

Perhaps the most significant characteristic of Hinduism, as it is one of the most difficult for the Occidental mind to grasp, is its utter divorce of morality and religion. The duties of life, says a recent writer, "are never inculcated in any Hindu temple, nor are any prayers ever offered for divine help in the performance of duty. It would be hard indeed even to conceive the possibility of prayer for purity being offered in a Hindu temple to a divinity surrounded by a bevy of dancing-girls." To meet with a devout Hindu who leads a flagrantly immoral life is a cause for no surprise or comment. The Hindu believes that a religious motive justifies every immorality, however gross. To abstain from certain meats and drinks, to avoid ceremonial defilement, are sacred duties, while lying and stealing and every form of deception are matters of indifference to the gods; indeed, immorality has their explicit sanction. The common failings of the

Hindu people are accordingly deceitfulness and immorality. Unhappily the government schools, while increasing the spread of knowledge, never touch upon ethics in any form, and have thus far proved powerless to elevate the moral tone of the people.

Public Worship

There is among the Hindus, aside from the great assemblies of the high festivals, no such thing as a worshipping and listening congregation. Hindu temples have no accommodations for such, the average temple being commonly only about ten feet square, just large enough for the image it shelters and the priest who officiates at the altar. None of them, not even the enormous pagodas of southern India, are arranged with a view to an audience. The people simply make their genuflexions and offerings, and pass on.

It must be understood that not all the gods in the Hindu system are worshipped alike in all parts of India. Each god has his own following, limited by locality, class, or sect, although many of the people adopt a large number of deities. Of the *Tri-murti*, Brahma, Siva, and Vishnu, the former is not often made a subject of worship; Siva is the ruling god in central and northwestern India; Vishnu is usually worshipped in one of his incarnations. Worshippers of Siva usually bear upon the forehead three horizontal marks made with white ashes. An upright mark, bright red, yellow, and white, stamps the follower of Vishnu.

The essence of religion in the popular mind is to punctiliously keep caste, and by "gaining merit" in various ways to ward off as many rebirths of the allotted eight millions as possible. Fear is the universally ruling principle in religion; its outworking the desire for propitiation.

Acquiring Merit

"A few," says one familiar with India by long residence, "an almost infinitesimal few, by austerities and prayers, are really seeking freedom from sin; but the masses of both high and low do not realize the disintegrating and decaying action of sin on the soul. Most are trying to propitiate the evil spirits, or bribe the better ones to grant temporal blessings."

Pilgrimages of incredible length and difficulty constitute a favorite method for "gaining merit." To journey on foot from the mouth of the sacred river Ganges to its source and back again, occupying six weary years, is supposed to secure extraordinary purification and favor with the gods.

Mohammedan Worship

In the Mohammedan mosque there are no idols, not even a symbolic suggestion, for the Mussulman is strictly non-idolatrous. Five times a day comes the impressive call to prayer, beginning with the first flush of dawn, "*Prayer is more than sleep — is more than sleep.*" Perhaps no class of men can be found more scrupulous in the performance of their religious forms than are the Mohammedans, but their religion leaves heart and character untouched, unchanged. Nevertheless, when compared with the disgusting rites of Hindu temples, the worship in a Moslem mosque presents a tranquillizing and almost spiritual semblance. Women are never admitted to the mosques.

It is said that the great difficulty in reaching Moslems with the message of the Gospel is their dislike, amounting to disgust, of the practical idolatry of the old churches of the East. Moslems abhor image worship, and in the old churches they behold pictures and images of Mary and the saints, before which the worshippers bow down in homage. This is abhorrent to the Moslem, and he associates this idolatry of the Greek and Roman branches of the Church with Christianity.

Buddhist Worship

The practice of the worship of Buddha in India is confined to the borders of Thibet, to Burma, and to Ceylon, and as it affects so small a portion of the Indian people, it must be left to the consideration of a succeeding volume. Buddhism in its outworking is but slightly in advance of Hinduism, since the images of Buddha are practically objects of idolatry, and the temple service is always accompanied by Nat or spirit-worship, while the spinning of prayer wheels and the flutter of prayer flags from poles and tree-tops bespeak its superstitious character. Certain superficial resemblances to Roman Catholicism are to be seen in Buddhism, such as the use of rosaries, the worship of relics, the prevalence of monasteries, and celibate orders of monks and nuns. The Buddhist priesthood is notoriously corrupt, and life in the monasteries has reached the point of depravity which has provoked complaint to the government. Buddhist temples are often on a vast and imposing scale, in contrast to the narrow shrines of Hinduism.

Parsi Customs regarding the Dead

The Parsis have been spoken of as a superior race in culture, intelligence, and aptitude for civilization. They retain, however, the most barbaric burial customs known perhaps to humanity. In broad, low towers, known as "Towers of Silence," in which iron grates are stretched to receive them, their dead are exposed naked, out of sight or reach of all living, to the ravages of the vultures which perch round the walls ready to gorge themselves in horrid greed upon their prey.

Thus even in the milder and less corrupt

forms of heathenism we find some abhorrent and depraved features. Everywhere in India is a strange lurking mystery of dark deeds; impassive apathy to suffering inconceivable to the Occidental mind; deep treachery, and unseen, unrecorded crime.

Caste

No influence is more potent in the bondage of the people to this darkened mind than is the mighty thraldom of caste. "On all sides you see the observance of minute caste rules," writes Margaret Denning. "You offer some bread or food to a hungry child; he refuses, but implores you to give him money, as he can buy raw grain and prepare it himself, so it will not be contaminated by your touch. Your cordial handshake is refused by the Zenana women for fear it will entail an extra bath of purification before they can prepare the next meal. Many castes dare not even receive a card from your hand. You must first lay it down, and then the other is free to lift it up." The caste system has extended in considerable measure to the Mohammedans, as in turn the Moslem seclusion of women has been taken on by the Hindus.

Among the major evils proceeding from caste are physical degeneracy, owing to the narrowing circles wherein marriage is permitted; the destruction of all sense of human brotherhood by the actual consecration of class hatred; the intellectual stagnation involved in the fact that the highest caste alone, the Brahmans, are considered fit to read and to teach.

The Brahmans

As laid down in the Code of Manu, the whole system of caste is but an organized scheme for the protection of the Brahmans in their colossal selfishness. "Since the Brahman sprang from the most excellent part, since he has the priority arising from primogeniture, and since he possesses the Veda, *he is by right the lord of this whole creation.*" (Code of Manu.)

The Brahmans are never in danger of poverty, as they have always been careful to make the efficacy of all rites which they administer dependent upon the gifts with which they are accompanied. In an emergency the Brahman is directed to obey the following rule: "Against misfortune let him preserve his wealth; at the expense of his wealth let him preserve his wife; but let him at all events preserve himself, even at the hazard of his wife and his riches."

There are four stages in the life of the Brahman as laid down in the Code of Manu: —

1. The investiture of the sacred thread, which signifies second birth, in his eighth year.
2. The married state.
3. The hermit life.
4. The devotee.

The sacred cord, in the case of the Brahman,

consists of three slender cotton threads, each consisting of three finer threads tightly twisted into one, and tied together in a sacred knot of peculiar construction. The cord is worn over the left shoulder and allowed to hang down diagonally across the body to the right hip. So soon as the Hindu boy has been made regenerate by the solemn putting on of this mystic symbol, his religious education and spiritual life are held to begin. It is only after he has been invested with the sacred thread that he has a right to the title "Twice-born," or can read or recite the Veda, or be known by the name Brahman.

The four original divisions of caste have been almost infinitely subdivided, the Brahman caste alone being divided into 1886 subcastes.

Yogis

There is in India a large class of devotees, drawn in part but by no means altogether from the Brahman caste. These ascetics do no work, do not teach, do good to no one. Their lives are spent in wandering from shrine to shrine, almost if not entirely naked, their bodies smeared with ashes, begging gifts. Self-inflicted cruelties of an appalling character are common among them; the most abnormal of these, hanging from hooks thrust through the flesh, has been prohibited by the English government. Most of these devotees have reduced themselves to a mental condition bordering on idiocy. The milder form of asceticism from which these fakirs have drawn their revolting practices is known as Yoga, a system of philosophy unworthy the name, the aim of which is the union of the human soul with the Supreme by the suppression of all thought, by intense concentration on nothing, and the constant repetition of the mystical word "Om."

Conclusion

As we look back over the conditions, racial, social, religious, here so rapidly sketched, India seems to lie before us, vast, dusky, unintelligible, peopled by swarming races of enfeebled men and oppressed women. Out of dimness and confusion incoherent voices reach us, wailing, mocking, imploring; spirits that peep and mutter flit through the gloom; famine, pestilence, and crime glide by like spectres; in mysterious temples silent priestesses attend upon rites which no man can name; cruelty, oppression, the lethargy of fatalism, lie like a pall over the great gray land. The spirit sinks under the almost hopeless gloom.

> "At last I heard a voice upon the slope
> Cry to the summit, 'Is there any hope?'
> To which an answer peal'd from that high land,
> But in a tongue no man could understand:
> And on the glimmering limit far withdrawn
> God made Himself an awful rose of dawn."

ILLUSTRATIVE SELECTIONS

Concerning the Beauties of Hinduism

The great majority of the population of India consists of idolaters, blindly attached to doctrines and rites which, considered merely with reference to the temporal interests of mankind, are in the highest degree pernicious. In no part of the world has a religion ever existed more unfavorable to the moral and intellectual health of our race. The Brahmanical mythology is so absurd that it necessarily debases every mind which receives it as truth; and with this absurd mythology is bound up an absurd system of physics, an absurd geography, an absurd astronomy. Nor is this form of paganism more favorable to art than to science. Through the whole Hindu pantheon you will look in vain for anything resembling those beautiful and majestic forms which stood in the shrines of ancient Greece. All is hideous and grotesque and ignoble. As this superstition is of all superstitions the most irrational and the most inelegant, so it is of all superstitions the most immoral. Emblems of vice are objects of public worship. The courtesans are as much a part of the establishment of the temple, as much the ministers of the gods, as the priests. Acts of vice are acts of public worship. Crimes against life, crimes against property, are not only permitted but enjoined by this odious theology. But for our interference, human victims would still be offered to the Ganges, and the widow would still be laid on the pile with the corpse of her husband, and burned alive by her own children. It is by the command and under the special protection of one of the most powerful goddesses that the Thugs join themselves to the unsuspecting traveller, make friends with him, slip the noose round his neck, plunge their knives into his eyes, hide him in the earth, and divide his money and baggage. — Lord Macaulay, Member of the Supreme Council of Calcutta, 1834–1838.

I have lived so long in a land where the people worship cows, that I do not make much of the differences which separate Christians from Christians.

—LORD MACAULAY.

WORDS OF A KASHMIRI PUNDIT

To live for three or four years in a society in which men and women meet, not as *masters* and *slaves*, but as friends and companions — in which feminine culture adds grace and beauty to the lives of men; to live in a society in which the prosaic hours of hard work are relieved by the companionship of a sweet and educated wife, sister, or mother, is the most necessary discipline required by our Indian youths in order that they may be able to shake off their old notions and to look upon an accomplished womanhood as the salt of human society which preserves it from moral decay. There is a very pernicious notion prevalent in India, that a free intercourse between the sexes leads to immorality. I confess that before I visited England I believed there was some truth in this notion. But now I believe no such thing. My own impression is that the chief safety-valve of public and private morality is the free intercourse between the sexes. This is the sore need of India, and we hope the *purdah* will soon be rent in twain and woman be emancipated.

LIFE IN THE ZENANA

I have lived in Zenanas and can speak from experience of what the lives of secluded women can be, — the intellect so dwarfed that a woman of twenty or thirty is more like a child, while all the worst passions of human nature are developed and stimulated; jealousy, envy, murderous hate, intrigue, running to such an extent that in some countries I have hardly ever been in a woman's house without being asked for drugs to disfigure the favorite wife, or take away her son's life. This request has been made of me nearly one hundred times.

—ISABELLA BIRD BISHOP.

Hinduism is perhaps the only system of belief that is worse than having no religion at all.

— DE TOCQUEVILLE.

NAUTCH GIRLS

"We wish to note with great pleasure and thankfulness that on the viceroy's tour through southern India he was nowhere greeted by the nautch girl. She used to be everywhere. It seemed as if we had lost the faculty of rejoicing in anything without dancing-girls. The nautch is a relic of the barbaric age, when greatness was measured by luxury and voluptuousness. It is devoutly to be wished that the precedent introduced in Lord Curzon's tour may be followed in all future receptions of viceroys and governors, and that India will show to the world how she can honor greatness without dishonoring womanhood.—From the *Indian Reformer*.

THE IDEAL HINDU WIFE

A wife is half the man, his truest friend,
A loving wife is a perpetual spring
Of virtue, pleasure, wealth; a faithful wife
Is his best aid in seeking heavenly bliss;
A sweetly speaking wife is a companion
In solitude, a father in advice,
A mother in all seasons of distress,
A rest in passing through life's wilderness.

— *Maha-bharata*.

Those believers who sit still at home, not having any hurt, and those who employ their fortune and their persons for the religion of God, shall not be held equal. God hath preferred those who employ their fortunes and their persons in that cause to a degree of honor above those who sit at home. — *Koran.*

Moslem and Hindu Worship

I once witnessed a very imposing spectacle in the great mosque at Delhi on the Moslem sabbath. Several hundred Indian Mohammedans were repeating their prayers in concert. They were in their best attire and fresh from their ablutions, and their concerted genuflections, the subdued murmur of their many voices, and the general solemnity of their demeanor, rendered the whole service most impressive. It contrasted strongly with the spectacle which I witnessed a little later in the temple of Siva, in Benares. The unspeakable worship of the linga; the scattering of rice and flowers, and the pouring of libations before this symbol; the hanging of garlands on the horns of sacred bulls, and that by women; the rushing to and fro tracking the filth of the sacred stables into the trodden ooze of rice and flowers which covered the temple pavements; the drawing and sipping of water from the adjacent cesspool known as the sacred well; the shouting and striking of bells, and the general frenzy of the people — all this could be considered as nothing short of wild and depraved orgies. If we must choose, give us Islam in contrast with the Siva worship of India. Yet Islam has no salvation, no scheme of grace, no great physician. — F. F. Ellinwood.

A Buddhist Shrine

Below us, to the right, in the rough Bhotia village, stands a little Buddhist temple, a common-looking native house, its single shabby inside room decked round with paintings black with age and unintelligible, its three tawdry idols hidden behind a glass, and half invisible in the darkness, its shelves of Buddhist scriptures thick with dust, its prayer wheels slowly grinding round "*Om-mam-padmi-hum.*"

Again in thought we stand upon the threshold watching the lined, dull, hopeless face of the priest as with a sweep of his hand he sets a row of prayer wheels, each about a foot in height, spinning like teetotums. In the entry stands a heavy, chestlike wheel, six or eight feet high, with two iron projections, which ring a bell each time it turns. The pleasant old wheel turner sets it in motion with an indifferent face, chanting as it slowly revolves. We glance into the dark interior, and back at the monotonous grinding of the great wheel with its bell, and the sing-song mechanical functions of the priests. A sense of the poverty and blindness of the faith these represent comes over us, and we think what it means that just such temples are the only houses of prayer to be found throughout Thibet, Bhotan, and Nepal.

— Lucy Guinness.

Interlude

Our cattle reel beneath the yoke they bear,
  The earth is iron and the skies are brass,
And faint with fervor of the flaming air
  The languid hours pass.

The well is dry beneath the village trees,
  The young wheat withers ere it reach a span,
And belts of blinding sand show cruelly
  Where once the river ran.

Pray, brothers, pray, but to no earthly king,
  Lift up your hands above the blighted grain,
Look westward; if they please, the gods shall bring
  Their mercy with the rain.

Look westward; bears the blue no brown cloud bank?
  Nay, it is written — wherefore shall we fly?
On our own field and by our cattle's flank
  Lie down, lie down to die. — RUDYARD KIPLING.

STARVING INDIA

The only persons of white blood in India who know what is actually going on are the missionaries, for they go about quietly everywhere, see everything, and cannot be deceived nor put off the scent by the native subordinates. . . . Yet what a missionary says would not be accepted by the government if it contradicted the reports of its own agents. . . . It was my great good fortune to be thrown with the missionaries from the start, and I was able to compare their methods and knowledge with those of the government people. It is as if you should sit with the audience in the front of a theatre and witness the performance from that point of view, and then should go behind the scenes and see the reality. The first is the posture of the government people; the latter that of the missionaries. It is the government's misfortune, not its fault.

* * * * * *

When I returned, after my tour to Bombay, and made the statement that eight million persons had already died of famine and disease directly caused thereby, I was met with blank incredulity. But I know, and the missionaries know, that the statement is within the truth. Eight millions — nearly twice the population of London! Think if you can of this number of persons slowly turning into skeletons and dying for lack of food — and no one knowing anything about it. And were it not for the heroic and unselfish efforts that England is making, this stupendous total would be multiplied by two or even three. — JULIAN HAWTHORNE.

THEMES FOR STUDY OR DISCUSSION

I. India's Great Famines and Plagues; their Causes and Preventive Measures.
II. Comparison between the Pearl Mosque at Agra (Mohammedan), the Shwe Dagon at Rangoon (Buddhist), and the Great Pagoda of Tanjore (Hindu), and their Respective Worships.
III. Hindu Characteristics: Physical, Mental, Moral.
IV. Famous Festivals and Pilgrimages.
V. Benares the Holy City and "Mother Gunga."
VI. Animal and Plant Worship.
VII. Everyday Life of English Residents.
VIII. Hindu and Mohammedan Social Customs; Marriage and Funeral Rites, etc.
IX. Life behind the Purdah or in the Zenana.
X. Village Life.
XI. Indian Arts and Crafts.
XII. The Attitude of the Indian Peoples toward their British Conquerors.

BOOKS OF REFERENCE

General Reference as before

Arnold's "India Revisited," V, VI, VII.
Chamberlain's "In the Tiger Jungle," III, X.
Denning's "Mosaics from India." For all but II, XII.
Lady Dufferin's "Our Vice-regal Life in India," III, VII, VIII, XI, XII.
Fergusson's "Indian Architecture," II.
Graham's "Great Temples of India, Ceylon, and Burma," II.
Guinness's "Across India," I, III, V, VIII, IX.
Hawthorne's Papers on India, *Cosmopolitan Magazine*, Vol. XXIII, for I, III, X.

Kipling's "Indian Tales," "Plain Tales from the Hills," "The Day's Work," I, III, V, VII, XII.
Kipling's "Kim," III, VIII, X, XII.
Kipling's Poems, III, VII, XII.
Leonowens's "Life and Travel in India," III, VII, VIII, IX.
Maxwell's "The Bishop's Conversion," VII.
Padmanji's "Once Hindu, now Christian," III, VI, VIII, X.
Rowe's "Everyday Life in India," I, IV, VIII, XI.
Russell's "Village Work in India," VIII, X, XI.
Savory's "British Sportswoman in India," III, VII, IX.
Steevens's "In India." For all but V, IX.
Thoburn's "India and Malaysia," III, VII, IX, XII.
Wilkins's "Daily Life and Work in India." For all but I, II, VII, XII.
Sir M. Williams's "Religious Life and Thought in India." For all but I, II, VII, XII.
Sir M. Williams's "India and the Indians," III, IV, VIII, X, XI.

IMPORTANT DATES IN THE HISTORY OF CHRISTIAN MISSIONS IN INDIA

1st Century A.D.	(Legendary.) The Apostle Thomas.
180–190 .	Pantænus.
300 *et seq.*	Nestorian Missions.
635 . . .	Three Persian Crosses.
640–1300	Islam supreme in Western Asia.
1321 . . .	The Four Martyrs of Thana.
1500 . . .	First Portuguese Missionaries.
1542 . . .	Francis Xavier.
1560 . . .	Introduction of the Inquisition into Portuguese Missions at Goa.
1600 . . .	Akbar, a Patron of Christianity.
1602–1642	Dutch Protestant Missions established.
1606–1693	The Jesuit Fathers of Madura.
1681 . . .	First English Church founded.
1705 . . .	First Danish Lutheran Missionary, Ziegenbalg.
1749 . . .	Schwartz, "the Christian."
1757 . . .	British Empire begun.
1788 . . .	David Brown plans the Church Mission.
1792 . . .	Formation of Baptist Missionary Society in England.
1793 . . .	William Carey sails for Calcutta.
1793–1813	Active Opposition of East India Company to the spread of the Gospel.
1800 . . .	First Hindu Convert baptized by Carey.
1805 . . .	Henry Martyn.
1812 . . .	First American Missionaries. Burma and Bombay.
1830 . . .	Alexander Duff.
1833 . . .	British Government declares itself neutral regarding Introduction of Christianity.
1835 . . .	American Presbyterian Missionaries enter the Punjab.
1850 . . .	First Medical Mission.
1856 . . .	First Methodist Mission in Bareilly.
1857 . . .	Martyrs of the Mutiny.
1859 . . .	First Call for Week of Prayer.
1861 . . .	Great Ingathering of Kols.
1870–1880	Great Ingathering of Telugus.
1886 . . .	The Student Volunteer Movement at Northfield, Mass.
1896 . . .	Formation of Student Volunteer Movement of India and Ceylon.

CHAPTER IV

THE INVASION OF LOVE

Later a sweet voice, *Love thy neighbor* said;
Then first the bounds of neighborhood outspread
Beyond all confines of old ethnic dread.

— SIDNEY LANIER.

WHILE Scythian, Arabian, Tatar, Persian, and European invaders, spurred on by lust of power, lust of blood, and lust of gold, were exploiting India for their own purposes, silently and without observation another invasion was going on. The great enlightener, Love, — love human and divine, — was shedding its rays athwart the thick darkness of India.

In foreign missions the church of Christ has found its touchstone, its supreme test, its ultimate vindication. The passion for humanity and the passion for God mingle here to form the noblest energy thus far expressed in terms of human action. In this adventure men and women who knew they had souls and were very sure of God, from the Apostolic age to the twentieth century, have filled up the measure of Christ's sufferings, laying down their lives, not for their friends, but for those who counted them aliens. They have not been the world's favorite heroes; but neither was their Lord.

At the foundation of this self-devotion lies the profound, unchangeable conviction of the Christian consciousness that the religion of Christ is not an ethnic religion, a religion for a single nation or for a peculiar phase of civilization, but a universal religion for every man in every age and every clime.

"What India needs," said a famous Hindu, "is Christ." Let us study how and by what manner of men Christ came to India.

I. APOSTOLIC AND ROMAN CATHOLIC MISSIONS

[In "Via Christi," the initial volume in this series, we have already become familiar with the achievements of the earliest heroes of Christian missions in India.]

St. Thomas

According to tradition, the Apostle Thomas, after the Day of Pentecost, carried the tidings of the world's redemption to India, and there suffered martyrdom. It is a well-established fact that two eminent Christian leaders named Thomas were known in southern India during the first centuries of the Christian era, and it is not impossible that Thomas Didymus did in very deed carry the gospel thither. The legend, however, lacks confirmation, although St. Thomas's Mount, near Madras, is popularly held to be the burial-place of the Apostle.

Roman, Jewish, and Christian Colonies

We have authentic basis for belief that a Jewish Christian colony existed in India from the latter part of the second century. In those days a Roman fleet sailed regularly once a year from a port on the Red Sea to India, and Jews and Jewish Christians going out by this route established settlements on the west coast. Hundreds of Roman coins have been discovered in South India, many of which bear the name of Augustus, and many more of Tiberius and other emperors, but of none later than Nero.

Pantænus

About 190 A.D. Pantænus, a learned and devout Christian of Alexandria, hearing that there was a community of Christians in India, resolved to visit them. It is certified that he reached the Malabar coast, and that he found among these Indian Christians the Hebrew or Aramaic gospel of St. Matthew. In 547 we have the interesting record of Cosmas, a merchant of Alexandria who visited India and wrote his impressions in a curious book called "Christian Topography." He testifies to the existence of Persian Christians in Ceylon, Socotra, and Malabar.

Syrian Christians

In the third century the Nestorian or Persian Christians established missions on the eastern or Coromandel coast of South India. A most interesting memorial of their work was discovered near Madras, and in an old church at Kottayam in 1547, in the shape of three Persian crosses bearing old Syriac inscriptions. The first-named is a slab bearing a cross in relief, built into the wall behind the altar in a church on St. Thomas's Mount. Those at Kottayam are similar. The inscriptions have been thus rendered into English: —

"*Let me not glory except in the cross of our Lord Jesus Christ who is the true Messiah and God alone and Holy Ghost.*"

These impressive witnesses, than which none could be more trustworthy, belong to the seventh century A.D. It will be noted that it was the coasts of South India, Malabar, and Coromandel which were earliest reached by the gospel. As a remnant of this pioneer missionary work, there still remain in India over three hundred thousand "Syrian Christians."

The conquest of India by the Mussulmans, beginning in the seventh century and continuing in the Mughal Empire throughout the Middle Ages, effectually checked the progress of Christianity.

Portuguese Roman Catholic Missions

In 1498 European invasion of India began with the Portuguese Vasco da Gama, and the year 1500 marks the beginning of Roman

Catholic missions. Let the student of the period of the Reformation in Europe in the sixteenth century bear in mind the part played by Spain in that bitter contest, and he will be prepared for the later developments of Portuguese evangelization.

Goa was the capital of Portuguese India, and became the seat of the bishopric and the centre of Roman Catholic influence. The Franciscans and Dominicans were early upon the scene, the first half of the fourteenth century being a time of great missionary activity among them.

Jordanus

The Dominican Jordanus stands out as a true and zealous missionary. He left a curious and interesting book entitled "The Wonders of the East," in which he describes the Parsis, the aborigines, the Hindu castes and idol worship, and the iconoclasm of the fierce Mohammedan invaders from the time of Sultan Mahmud. A strange prophetic belief among the natives he thus indicates, "The pagans of this India have prophecies of their own that we Latins are to subjugate the whole world."

Four Martyrs of Thana

The martyrdom of the companions of Jordanus, the four young "wrestlers for Christ,"—Thomas, James, Demetrius, and Peter, at Thana,—in 1321, by the Mohammedans, forms a noble and pathetic episode in the annals of Romish missions in India. Odoric the Bohemian, a wandering missionary, carried the ashes of the four martyrs on his journeyings in Asia for fourteen years.

Francis Xavier

The worst and the best of Roman Catholic missionary energy is condensed into the passionate, self-sacrificing, but imperious genius of St. Francis Xavier.

This famous Jesuit saint landed at Goa, May 6, 1543, in his thirty-seventh year. The story of his going through the streets ringing a bell to call the people to come out to hear him preach is familiar. For three years Xavier toiled devotedly as a missionary in South India, baptizing thousands, among whom were a large number of infants to whom he eagerly desired to extend the saving grace of the sacrament. Xavier's whole line of action was based on this theory, and to it is owing the large number of nominal converts enrolled by him.

The Inquisition in India

In 1545 Xavier requested of John III of Portugal the favor of introducing the inquisition into his Indian dominions. This was done in 1560, and it continued in action with its customary diabolical cruelty until 1816. Xavier died on the 2d of December, 1552, on the barren island of Sanchian near Canton, China. His body, after various burials and removals, was taken to Goa, and is here still safely kept (supposedly), being exhibited as a sacred relic from time to time.

Philip II of Spain, who in 1595 had gained supremacy over Portugal, sent Menezes as archbishop to Goa. His name has been made infamous by his persecution of the Nestorian Christians.

Akbar and Christianity

About the end of the sixteenth century, Geronimo Xavier, nephew of Francis, made his way from the Portuguese settlements north and east as far as Agra. This was in the time of the mighty Akbar, who, having among his wives a Christian convert, manifested a pronounced interest in the tenets of Christianity, and employed Xavier to write for him a history of Christ and Peter. As it is said of Akbar that he listened impartially to the arguments of the Brahman and the Mussulman, the Fire worshipper, the Jew, the Jesuit, and the sceptic, this fact was rather an incident than an event.

The Malabar Scandals

Among the successors of Xavier in South India were Robert de Nobili and John de Britto, who devised and carried out a scheme of imposture for securing the conversion of the Hindus, as strange as it was ill-judged. Mastering the Hindu philosophy and ritual, and the native dialects by long study and in strictest seclusion, they reappeared in Madras, claiming to be in one case a Brahman prince, in the other an incarnation of Brahma. These claims, sustained for a long period, supported by forgeries, constitute the famous Malabar scandals. De Britto died a victim to the rage of the Brahmans.

Progress of Romanism in India

Romanism, in spite of rents and schisms, has made great progress in India, chiefly in Madras and Bengal, and its adherents outnumber Protestant Christians almost two to one. Its spectacular ritual and processions, its sacrifice of the mass, its profusion of images, pictures, and symbols, its prayers to numberless patron saints presiding over specific departments of life, and above all its ascetic priesthood and virgin worship, combine to make its appeal a comparatively easy one to the followers of Brahmanism. Both systems have the common characteristic of combining the subtlest mysticism of theory with gross idolatry of practice. The Roman Catholic clergy of Hindustan comprise an archbishop of Goa, nineteen bishops who are vicars apostolic, and nearly nine hundred priests. The church has been divided in allegiance between Portuguese dominance and the Propaganda of Rome.

II. EARLY PROTESTANT MISSIONS

Dutch Indian missions were wholly Protestant, and are contemporaneous with the rise of Dutch Oriental commerce; but they seem in these earlier centuries to have been strangely mingled with commercial methods and motives, and were without permanent value. The process of making converts was conducted "in blocks," the natives being forced for support to confess Christianity, and receiving baptism by the thousand, with no evidence of sincerity. When, in 1796, the English overpowered the Dutch in India, there were nearly half a million professed converts of the Dutch Reformed Church in Ceylon; but in 1850 it is said that not a single congregation remained.

Danish Missions

While Portuguese Jesuits were disgracing the name of Christ by their fantastic frauds and fanatical persecutions, while Holland was following a futile commercial policy of wholesale evangelization, Denmark was quietly laying in its eastern possessions the foundation of the great missionary movement of to-day in purity of faith and righteousness. The inception of this work was due to the earnest efforts of Dr. Lütkens, court chaplain to Frederick IV, who set before the king the duty of giving the gospel to his Indian dependency.

While the Danish Mission, as such, did not prove permanent, owing, perhaps, to the toleration of caste customs in converts, it exerted a lasting influence, laid a strong foundation for the work of Carey and his associates, and was made forever glorious by the names of the great Lutheran missionaries—Ziegenbalg, Plütschau, and Schwartz.

The first centre of the Danish movement was Tranquebar, on the Madras coast, where, among the Tamil people, Ziegenbalg and Plütschau began their work in 1706. These devoted men were not, however, Danes, but German-Lutherans, for Lütkens failed to find in all Denmark men ready and fitted for such a work. "Seek, then, for men in Germany," said Frederick IV. In Werder, twenty miles from Berlin, hard at work in his parish, was found the right man, Bartholomew Ziegenbalg. Plütschau, a man of like mind, was named to be his companion by Francke of Halle, and both accepted the appointment as a call from God. They were later joined by Gründler and Schultze, who completed the work of translation of the whole Bible into Tamil, the first Indian Bible, in 1727, two hundred years after Luther made his translation. Ziegenbalg, who died at thirty-six, had completed the translation of the New Testament, and left behind a grammar and dictionary of the Tamil tongue. His name must forever shed lustre on the Lutheran Church of Germany, as that of a second great pioneer of Biblical translation.

The efforts of German Lutherans under Danish patronage, "the Halle missionaries," as they are called, were continued by the greatest of them all, the immortal "Father Schwartz," whose portrait has been vividly drawn for us in "Via Christi." He extended the work to Tanjore, and before the dawn of the nineteenth century there were forty thousand converts in the Tranquebar Mission. With the death of Schwartz, 1798, ends the first and preparatory period of Protestant missions in India.

III. ATTITUDE OF THE EAST INDIA COMPANY TOWARD CHRISTIANIZATION OF INDIA

It will be noted by reference to the chronological table at the beginning of this chapter, that Portuguese missions were nearly three hundred years old, Dutch nearly two hundred, and that nearly a century elapsed after the period of the first Danish missionary before England made its initial movement toward Christianizing India.

Meanwhile the English had become supreme through a large part of South India, having expelled the last ensign of the French nation from the Coromandel coast; Plassey had been fought; the presidencies of Madras, of Calcutta, and of Bombay were securely British, and many other provinces were tributary, while Lord Cornwallis, as governor-general of India, was reviving in pomp and power (1786–1793) traditions of the reign of the Mughal Emperor Aurangzeb.

East India Company and Idolatry

It would naturally have been expected that the rise into supremacy of a power so thoroughly Christian and Protestant as that of the British would from the first have brought Christianity and its moral standards in its train. The monopoly under Clive of the opium traffic; the notorious favoring of heathenism as a part of the avowed policy of the East India Company of non-interference with native religion; the official maintenance of heathen temples and honoring of idols, and the systematic repression of all missionary labor, are the strange and unnatural facts which confront us. The selfish and cynical attitude of the East India Company's government toward the religious condition of its new empire can be summed up in Gibbon's words concerning the old Roman Empire, "The various religions were regarded by the people as equally true, by the philosophers as equally false, by the government as equally profitable."

William Wilberforce

In the midst of the material selfishness of his people and time towers the form of William Wilberforce, who led the great struggle in the

British Parliament which, in 1813, resulted in an act stating that "such means shall be employed as are calculated for the introduction of useful knowledge among the natives of India and for their moral and religious elevation." Even so mild and inoffensive a measure as this was carried through against stubborn resistance, and while a few missionaries were admitted at this time, the government steadily refused to admit others until 1833. At this time the government also by a charter put a stop to official endowment of idolatry, and declared itself explicitly "neutral," meaning that while it would not suppress idolatry, it would no longer support it.

Chaplains of the Anglican Church

The first English church was founded in Calcutta in 1681 for English residents; a few chaplains of the Church of England were sent out through the century following, and the Danish Protestant missionaries were tolerated. The English chaplains unfortunately were frequently men of careless life and unworthy character, and the conduct of the great mass of the English was such as to lead the natives to believe Christianity the religion of the devil. It is an old proverb among Anglo-Indians that "the Ten Commandments cease to be in force beyond the Isthmus of Suez." During this long, dark period there were among the chaplains of the East India Company five exceptional men whose names deserve to be held in lasting remembrance: these were David Brown, Claudius Buchanan, Henry Martyn, Thomas Thomason, and Daniel Corrie. These earnest and consecrated East Indian chaplains were mainly protégés of Charles Simeon of Cambridge, the greatest evangelical leader in the Anglican Church in his day. Among them the name of Henry Martyn always shines with peculiar lustre, by reason of his unconquerable spirit valiantly struggling with physical weakness, his surpassing religious genius, and his early death. In this connection we may make mention of Reginald Heber, second bishop of the See of Calcutta at a later date (from 1822 to 1826), who united the zeal and piety of the Christian with the accomplishments of the scholar and the gentleman. Few men have ever won in equal measure the general esteem of society in India.

IV. MISSIONS IN INDIA FROM 1793 TO 1857

Discouraged by public sentiment at home and the prohibitive policy of the company on the field, English missionaries were late in appearing. But their advent in India, when at last it came, by common consent, marks the actual beginning of the great Protestant missionary movement of modern times. The name of the first English missionary, William Carey, is the most illustrious in the annals of Protestant missions; and the English Church Missionary Society (the C. M. S.), representing the evangelical wing of that body, is to-day the strongest and most efficient organization of its kind in the world.

The English were worth waiting for; and well did Southey say, "The first step toward winning the natives to our religion is to show them that we have one."

The Serampore Triad,— Carey, Marshman, and Ward

The determination of William Carey, the "consecrated cobbler" (himself a Baptist), to preach the gospel to the Hindus, led to the formation, in 1792, of the Baptist Missionary Society. Appointed by the society as its first missionary, Carey, then in his thirty-third year, sailed for India, June 13, 1793, accompanied by a Christian surgeon, John Thomas. At this time all Europeans not in public service were forbidden to set foot in the East India Company's territories in India without especial license. So inflexible was the official opposition to the entrance of missionaries that Carey and Thomas, in order to avoid expulsion, were obliged, on arrival in Calcutta, to register as indigo planters and to engage in that occupation. "There," says Eugene Stock, "and in that capacity, lived for six years Carey, the one representative in India of the missionary zeal of Christian England; and in that obscure — one may say ignominious — way began English missions in her great dependency." In 1799 Joshua Marshman and William Ward, with others, under appointment by the English Baptist Society, landed in Calcutta; but being instantly ordered to leave the country, they took refuge in the friendly Danish settlement of Serampore, sixteen miles above Calcutta, on the right bank of the Hughli River. Here they were soon joined by Carey, glad to escape from British hostility, and the great "Serampore Triad" was formed. In 1800 the first Hindu convert, Krishna Pal, was baptized. The Serampore men, who may be justly regarded as missionary statesmen and apostles, broke wellnigh every path which has since become a highroad of missionary activity. They laid the foundation for almost every method of subsequent missionary endeavor, whether in school or college, in organizing native preachers and lay workers, or in exercising the right of petition against the crimes committed in the name of the Hindu religion. Above all, however, ranks their distinguished and scholarly labor in translating the Bible into the vernacular. In view of their limited education, their marvellous attainments in this particular suggest an especial divine endowment. Carey, whose success as a translator has won for him the title of "the Wycliffe of the East," completed a Bengali dictionary in three volumes, and translated the Bible, or some of its parts, into thirty-six dialects. He prepared grammars and dictionaries in the Sanskrit, Marathi, Bengali, Punjabi, and Telugu dialects. His fame as a botanist was second only to his reputation as a linguist. His whole long residence of forty-one years in India proved him a man of extraordinary intellectual power, accompanied with the rarest humility and most unfaltering devotion to his master, Jesus Christ, and with a consuming love for his fellow-men. Financially the Serampore Triad did what no three men since have done — contributed by their efforts to the cause of missions and India's elevation nearly half a million dollars, and this when the brotherhood of three families lived at the same table at a cost of five hundred dollars a year. It can fairly be said that the conceptions of Carey and his associates as to the introduction of Christianity among a pagan people have for a century dominated Protestant missions.

(1) Missionary organizations beginning work in India previous to 1857.

Thus we see that the English Baptists entered India in 1793; the Congregationalists followed in 1798; the Church of England took up the work in 1807; the American Board, representing the Congregationalists of the United States, in 1812; the American Baptists in 1814, and the English Methodists the same year. The common origin of the American

Board and the Baptist Missionary Union demand especial notice, as being the first of all American Protestant missionary organizations, and thus marking an epoch.

When, in 1810, at the Theological Seminary at Andover, the "haystack" missionary heroes,—Mills, Richards, Rice, and Hall,—met Adoniram Judson, a memorial was drawn up, signed by him and three others, asking the General Association of Massachusetts "whether they might expect patronage and support from a missionary society in this country, or must commit themselves to the direction of an European Society." The result was the formation of the American Board of Commissioners for Foreign Missions in 1812, representing the American Congregationalists (A. B. C. F. M.), under whose auspices Hall, Nott, Rice, Judson, and Newell sailed for India. Two years later the avowal by Judson of his change of views on the subject and mode of baptism, and his own baptism at Calcutta, led to the creation of the American Baptist Missionary Union (A. B. M. U.).

The earliest mission of the American Board was that at Bombay, founded by Gordon Hall and his colleagues. From here the work has extended to Poona, Ahmednagar, Satara, and Sholapur, and is now known as the Marathi Mission. The Ceylon Mission, begun in 1816 at Tillipally and Batticotta by Poor, Richards, and Meigs, is one of the firmest, strongest, and most thorough in India, and is preëminent for the character of its schools, and especially for Jaffna College, founded in 1872. The Madura Mission, among the Tamil people, was begun in 1834 and is doing a noble work, largely of an educational character. Madras is the seat of the Tamil publishing work. The American Board has furnished India with many of its most distinguished, scholarly, and successful missionaries. In 1850 Rev. H. M. Scudder, M.D., son of John Scudder, having labored in connection with the American Board for some years, made a tour with Mr. Dulles of South India with a view to establishing an out-station. The result was the mission to Arcot, forever identified with the great Scudder family. Eight sons of Dr. John Scudder and many grandsons and granddaughters have devoted their lives to the salvation both of soul and body of India's millions. The Arcot Mission has passed into the hands of the Dutch Reformed Church of the United States.

American Baptist missions in India from the first were definitely confined to three vast but distinct regions. Of these the first, Burma, was visited by English Baptists, Chater, Mardon, and Felix Carey, as early as 1807; but it was with the coming of Adoniram Judson, "the greatest of American missionaries," in 1813, that the work of evangelization really began. The genius of its founder, the exquisite personality of Ann H. Judson, and the pathos of her noble life and of that of Sarah Boardman Judson, have cast a halo of unparalleled romance over this mission. Judson laid a foundation broad and deep, on which a mighty superstructure has risen in this seat of Buddhism. At his death there were over seven thousand native Christians. Among about thirty stations the following may be named as most important,—Rangoon, Maulmein, Bassein, Henzada, Toungoo, and Mandalay. Judson's translation of the whole Bible into Burmese is a work of the highest permanent value.

A most interesting feature of the Burmese Mission is the work among the Karens. This people number many tribes (among whom are the Sgau Karens and Pwo Karens), for all of which the American Baptists carry on missions. The work was begun in 1828 by George Dana Boardman of the A. B. M. U. The first disciple to be baptized was Ko-thah-byu, formerly a slave of reckless, dangerous character, who became by the mighty regenerating power of God a faithful, humble laborer for the conversion of his race. The death of Boardman, after his brief but noble term of service, forms a singularly pathetic event. The persecution of Christian Karens in 1852 by the Burmans, and the heroic devotion of Justus Vinton and his wife, are episodes of marked interest. There are now about five hundred Karen churches in Burma, with thirty-five thousand members, thousands having confessed Christ under Vinton's ministrations. They are distinguished for their zeal, their steadfastness under persecution, and their spirit of self-help. They have built and endowed a hospital; have endowed their own high school, "the best in all Burma;" their churches are kept under strict discipline; their pastors are thoroughly trained; the system of benevolence reaches *every church member*, and all in all they compare favorably with the country churches of the United States.

In Assam, to which the eminent Nathan Brown went in 1836, the Baptists labor almost alone among the Garo, Naga, Kanari, and other aboriginal tribes, doing a great printing work in native dialect at Sibsagor, and holding six other important stations, with sixty-nine churches, most of which are self-supporting. Perhaps the most noteworthy achievement in Assam has been the reduction to writing by the missionaries of six different languages hitherto without alphabet.

The third Baptist territory, as it may be called, is in southeastern India, among the Telugu people, with Madras, Ongole, and Nellore as centres. Work was begun here also in 1836, by Samuel Day, and was carried on later by Lyman Jewett. The Nellore Mission, the centre of the Telugu work, remained so unproductive for seventeen years that the missionary Union in 1853 was on the point of formally abandoning it, at their annual meeting at Albany, N. Y., when a thrilling hymn, naming Nellore the "Lone Star Mission," written by Dr. S. F. Smith, the author of "America," caused a sudden revulsion of feeling, and it was unanimously voted to reënforce the mission. Events have more than justified this action, as the great revivals under John E. Clough, which began in 1867, and reached their climax ten years later, have rendered the Telugu work one of the most marvellous mass movements in the history of Indian missions. In a single day 1000 brought their idols to the missionaries in Ongole to be destroyed, on another day 2222 were baptized, and at one time 8691 within the space of ten days.

Ceylon was an early field, being first entered by Protestants in 1812, when English Baptists began their work at Colombo, being reënforced later by English Wesleyans as well as by the missionaries of the American Board.

In 1835 the Freewill Baptist Society of the United States sent out four missionaries,—Mr. Noyes and Mr. Phillips and their wives, who planted a station in Orissa. In this province much admirable work has been done, notably the reduction of the Santal tongue to a written language by Mr. Phillips, for which he received the thanks of the British government. Centres have been established at Balasore, Jellasore,

Midnapore, and other points. At Jellasore an asylum has been founded for sick and suffering pilgrims. The work abounds in interesting features.

The German Lutheran Society of America in 1842, four years after the death of the noble Rhenius, selected the Kistna district, north of Nellore, as a field of labor. While this society owed its origin to the unfortunate complication of Lutheran missionaries working under Episcopal authority, and the misunderstanding arising therefrom, their course of action was thoroughly Christian and magnanimous, and their work has been one of marked power and fruitfulness. Their first missionary, Heyer, settled at Guntur. It will be observed that these early missionary organizations were all established on strictly denominational lines, as seemed unavoidable according to the spirit of the time, when great emphasis was laid upon divisive distinctions. One striking, although in the end unsuccessful, exception must be noticed. The London Missionary Society was formed in 1795, three years later than the Baptist Missionary Society which owed its life to Carey's call. This later society was formed by a union of Presbyterians, Independents, and members of the Church of England, and it gave out the following manifesto: "That its design is not to send Presbyterianism, Episcopalianism, or any other form of church government (about which there may be differences of opinion among serious persons), but the glorious gospel of the blessed God to the heathen, and that it shall be left (as it ought to be left) to the minds of the persons whom God may call to the fellowship of his Son from among them, to assume for themselves such church government as to them shall appear most agreeable to the word of God."

This plan of procedure, thus nobly stated, failed through the withdrawal after a time of the Episcopalians and Presbyterians.

In 1834 began the labor of the Basel Mission in Malabar. In 1835 American Presbyterian missions were begun at Ludhiana, in the Punjab, by John C. Lowrie and William Reed, reënforced in 1849 by James Wilson, C. W. Forman, and the illustrious John Newton. Forman spent forty-six, Newton fifty-six, years in India, and both have left an indelible impress on the Punjab. The Presbyterian Church now carries on three important missions,—Ludhiana, Farukhabad (started at Allahabad), and the Western India Mission. The medical work is especially remarkable, and there are institutions for lepers at Sabatha, Ambala, and Saharanpur. The first was established by John Newton. The hospitals at Miraj, Allahabad, Ambala, and Ferozepore are finely equipped and manned. Other important stations in the Punjab are Fategarh, Lahore,

Dehra Dun, and Jullunder. There are five presbyteries. In the year 1856 Isidor Lowenthal, a converted Polish Jew and a graduate of Princeton, pushed the work up toward the Afghan frontier as far as Peshawar. A distinguished Brahman convert, Kali Chatterjee, has for years conducted work at Hoshyarpore. John H. Morrison, of the Ludhiana Mission, was known as "The Lion of the Punjab," by reason of the fearlessness of his preaching; while of John Newton it was said, "He was one of the holiest and best-beloved men the Punjab has ever seen."

In 1841 the Leipsic Lutherans established work in the Carnatic, the Irish Presbyterians in Gujerat, the Welsh Calvinists in Bengal, and the Berlin Mission in Behar.

In 1846 the German Mission to the Kols of Chota Nagpore, two hundred miles west of Calcutta, was started.

In 1855 the Moravians established their mission in Kyelang, in the foothills of the Himalayas, where they have done most valuable and heroic work. The fact that in this body of Christians one out of every fifty-eight communicants is a foreign missionary gives them a place of noble distinction in Christendom.

The Scotch United Presbyterians began their labors in 1855 in the province of Rajputana, a province more extensive in area than Great Britain and Ireland, and the seat of the Rajputs, the famous hereditary Aryan chieftains. Their work has extended from Rajputana into the adjacent province of Gujerat. Dr. Shoolbrel, a man of light and leading, was their pioneer. Their work centres about Jeypore, Ajmere, Deoli, and Beawar. In the same year American United Presbyterians entered the Punjab, Sialkot being the first station. The work now comprises eight districts, and is carried on with great effectiveness by a force of twelve ordained and twelve women missionaries. The theological seminary and memorial hospital at Sialkot are effective features.

In 1856 William Butler, the great pioneer of American Methodists in India, arrived in Calcutta, and proceeded to Rohilkhand, between the upper Ganges and the Himalayas. Hardly, however, had he become settled in his station of Bareilly when the Sepoy Mutiny broke out, and on the 31st of May, 1857, the English residents were all put to death or put to flight by the Sepoys. Dr. Butler and his family escaped to Naina Tal, another mountain town of the Himalayas, and for a long time disappeared from view. The little group were known for months as "the Naina Tal Refugees."

In 1858 the American Dutch Reformed Church, whose earliest representative had been John Scudder, sent out by the American Board, came into the field with vigor and zeal. Arcot is the region of their large activity.

(2) Early Heroes.

Out of the noble army of pioneer missionaries, during the period from Carey to the Mutiny (1793–1857), we can single out but a few of the most illustrious names besides those already mentioned. Alexander Duff, who in 1830 arrived in Calcutta as the first missionary of the Established Church of Scotland, and became the founder of English education in India, is estimated by Bishop Thoburn as the most prominent man in the missionary world after William Carey.

Other great names are those of Charles Rhenius (1814), "one of the ablest, most clear-sighted, practical, and zealous missionaries whom India has ever seen"; Daniel Poor, who in 1816 began his fruitful labors in the island of Ceylon; Eugenio Kincaid, the fearless missionary, explorer, and envoy; the Bombay missionaries, Donald Mitchell (1825), Dr. J. Murray Mitchell, Robert Nesbit, and John Wilson (1835), of the Free Church of Scotland; Robert T. Noble (1814), of the English Church Missionary Society, who founded at Masulipatam the college which has been called "the Cambridge of South India"; Stephen Hislop, founder of Hislop Missionary College at Nagpur; and that other mighty Scotchman, John Anderson, the apostolic successor, after the spirit, of Alexander Duff, who carried his methods to Madras, and who died "such a death as I have never before witnessed," said one of his physicians. "His constitution should have borne another twenty years of labor, but he was broken with the weight of heavy responsibilities and exhausting toil without respite, while practising the most rigid self-denial that in every way the work might be advanced." Truly this might be adopted as the typical missionary epitaph.

Time would fail to tell of many more, apostles and martyrs, who through faith wrought righteousness, obtained promises, and subdued kingdoms.

V. RAPID SURVEY OF INDIAN MISSIONS FROM THE MUTINY TO THE PRESENT TIME

"The history of Christian India," says Smith, "began in the year 1858,"—the Annus Mirabilis of modern missions. The Sepoy Mutiny, in 1857, opened a new period. The timid, untried, native Christians were identified by the mutineers with the governing class and put to the test of martyrdom for their Master's sake.

Martyrs of the Mutiny

Thirty-seven missionaries and their families were butchered, and an unknown number of native Christians. "The Mohammedans always, and the Hindus occasionally, offered such their lives as the price of denying their Lord. Not one instance can be cited of failure to confess him by men and women, very often of frail physique, and but yesterday of the same faith as their murderers." Happily the records of the infant church of India contain a narrative of one survivor of the torture of that time, Gopinath Nundy, a Brahman converted under Alexander Duff. This heroic recital is given us in Smith's "Conversion of India."

Among the martyrs were the Presbyterian missionaries stationed at Farukhabad, Freeman, Johnson, McMullen, Campbell, and their wives and the two little children of the Campbells. They were captured as they tried to escape down the Ganges to Cawnpore, and at Nana Sahib's orders were all taken to the parade-ground and shot in cold blood. How calmly they met the end these words of Mrs. Freeman's, written just before her death, show:—

"We are in God's hands and we know that He reigns. We have no place to flee for shelter—but under the covert of His wings, and there we are safe. . . . Should I be called to lay down my life, most joyfully would I die for Him who laid down His life for me."

New consecration, vigor, and purpose were infused into every missionary society laboring in India, as they saw of what stuff their converts were made; while Queen Victoria's Proclamation, in which the crown assumed direct responsibility of the empire, doing away with the shifting and mercenary "John Company,"

M

and assuring all her subjects equal and impartial protection, stimulated new organizations to enter new fields.

Origin of the Week of Prayer

Close following the agitation of the Mutiny came a call from the Presbyterian Mission at Ludhiana to the whole Christian Church to unite in an annual Week of Prayer, to begin with January 8, 1859; "that all God's people of every name and nation, of every continent and island be . . . invited to unite with us in the petition that God would now pour out His Spirit upon all flesh, so that all the ends of the earth might see His salvation."

Such was the origin, such the missionary motive, too often forgotten, of the Week of Prayer. It was John H. Morrison who first conceived the thought and put it in action.

Methodist Progress

Most stimulating is the broad onward sweep of the Methodists in India, with their great names of Butler, Parker, Taylor, Thoburn, and many more.

Emerging from their hiding, the Naina Tal refugees, upon whom the intense interest of all their brethren in America was concentrated, proceeded to establish themselves in Mordarabad and Lucknow. In 1864 the bounds of their work were extended so as to take in southern and eastern Oudh and other adjacent regions, their field being included in a triangle bounded on the west by the Ganges, on the southeast by a line drawn from the city of Allahabad eastward to the Himalayas and by the great Snow Mountains on the north and northeast. The year 1870 marked another crisis, when Bishop Thoburn carried the work westward across the Ganges. Bishop Taylor's masterly evangelistic genius, and the revival under him in South India, made new centres in Bombay, in Poona, in Secunderabad, in Madras, and in Calcutta. The work was then pushed eastward as far as Rangoon, Methodists thus coming to share with Baptists and Anglicans the work of evangelizing Burma; points of vantage were seized in the Punjab and in the Central Provinces,—in fine, instead of the compact triangle at first occupied, the Methodist body now surveys all India as its field. In 1892, in the North India Conference more than nineteen thousand were baptized. "To-day," said Dr. Gracey recently to the writer, "a hundred thousand natives are ready to cast away their idols and profess Christ. If we had but teachers in whose hands to place them for Christian training, we could baptize that number at once." "We entered Calcutta in 1872," says Bishop Thoburn, "without a dollar in the shape of financial resources. We had not a member in all that great city to receive us. Bishop Taylor preached for months in a suburban chapel kindly placed at his disposal by a Baptist missionary, but his labors for the most part were confined to private houses. We held on, and now we have the largest place of worship, not only in Calcutta, but in India, and the largest congregation."

German and English Success

Another stirring chapter of history is furnished us by the extraordinary success of the German Mission among the Kols, the aboriginal people of Chota Nagpore. At the end of 1861 there were 2400 converts. Ten years later there were 20,727, and at the present time there are 30,000.

Founded early in the century by the gifted, but erratic and mysterious Ringletaube, the great Tamil missions in Travancore, under the London Missionary Society, have made phenomenal progress. In the decade 1861–1871 they added 10,000 to the number of converts, and more than 8000 between 1871–1881, bidding fair to evangelize the entire region. Strong missions are also sustained by this Society in North and South India.

Work of the Anglican Church

While the Protestant Episcopal Church of America has not thus far made itself markedly felt in India, the Church of England is the state church, sustained at a cost of about eight hundred thousand dollars annually. The prestige of the establishment is naturally thus transmitted, and the Anglican clergy are found in all important towns, and occupy many positions of influence. The C. M. S. (Church Missionary Society) and S. P. G. (Society for the Propagation of the Gospel), the one representing low and the other high church sympathies, have undoubtedly done the most efficient work of any branch of the Christian church in India. The province of Tinnevelly, at the southern extremity of the peninsula, stands foremost as the most Christianized province of India. About 1822 Bishop Heber wrote: "The strength of the Christian cause in India is in these missions, Tinnevelly and Tanjore; it will be a grievous and heavy sin if England and the agents of her bounty do not nourish and protect the churches here founded."

This mission, originally known as the Palamcotta Mission, dates back to the time of the Danish Lutheran missionaries of Tranquebar, and was visited by the celebrated Schwartz in 1778. After coming under German Lutheran oversight, notably that of Rhenius, in 1820, it was finally adopted by the English societies above named. Under their control a period of wonderful expansion has ensued, particularly within the last quarter century. The first missionary bishops or coadjutors of the Bishop of Madras were chosen from the Tinnevelly missions, which, in 1890, numbered sixty thousand Christians. Rhenius, who has been called bolder and more talented even than Schwartz himself, originated the policy of forming his native Christians into separate villages. This method is successfully followed to-day in the work of the American United Presbyterians in the Punjab.

Canadian and Other Societies

Canadian Baptists began work in the Kistna district at Coconada in 1874, and have since planted several stations in the Vizagapatam district on the northern Madras coast. The Presbyterian Church of Canada founded a Foreign Missionary Society in 1875, and has stations at Gwalior, Indore, Ratlam, and other points in central and north India.

In central India, at Hoshangabad, English Friends began their work in 1874. Earnest and thorough teaching is imparted, and five centres are held by an efficient working force. Orphanages for both boys and girls, with nearly a thousand inmates, form an interesting feature of this work. American Friends have very recently undertaken a mission at Nowgong, Assam.

Educational Work

From the period of Carey and Duff no feature has been more emphasized in Indian missions than the education of natives as the basis for evangelization. "Previous to the arrival of Alexander Duff in Calcutta, in 1830, Christian education had been mainly carried on in the vernacular. Dr. Duff with all his vigor entered energetically into extensive educational reforms. Taking advantage of the desire on the part of the natives for a knowledge of English, and convinced that the Hindu mind, if well educated in science, history, and philosophy, must refuse to believe the principles of Hinduism, he established the Mission College at Calcutta on a broad educational basis."

All who visit India, whether Christian or agnostic, agree that the best antidote for the superstition and degradation of the people is the spread of knowledge. But the non-Christian education furnished by government schools has failed to produce any moral improvement. Conscious of this, the government has of late encouraged the religious societies at work in the country to establish schools of their own. An imposing array of divinity schools, colleges, seminaries, high schools, English, vernacular, boarding, and day schools, kindergarten and primary, deaf-mute, blind, manual training, etc., all on a Christian basis, now stand as a powerful factor in civilizing and Christianizing "Young India." Closely allied with this department is the work of translation and its right hand, — the printing-press. The indispensable character of this part of the work is self-evident, and is attested by the prominence given to its press work by each society engaged in Indian missions.

Medical Work

No greater blessing has been conferred by the American churches on British India than that of modern medical missions, first tentatively and successfully practised by Dr. John Scudder (1819), of the Dutch Reformed Church, and now adopted by all the societies as a prominent feature of their work.

The early labors of John Thomas, colleague of Carey, had not been taken up by the English, and this branch of labor had been arrested for a time. The first regular medical mission of India was established by Dr. H. M. Scudder, son of John Scudder, in 1850, in North Arcot. Most interesting is the story of Dr. Colin Valentine, who, "by means of his medical skill exercised in the successful treatment of the Ranee of Jeypore, wife of the Maharajah, gained access, both for himself and his brother missionaries, to one of the most bigoted and exclusive strongholds of idolatry in northern India, where the United Presbyterian Church has now a prosperous mission."

Native medical practice has been notoriously inadequate and pernicious, and perhaps no country affords a sadder spectacle of diseased and mutilated humanity than does India. Dr. Duff first induced his Bengali students to take full medical qualifications in Great Britain. Indian universities now give requisite medical training, and a new order of intelligent practice in hospitals and dispensaries has been ushered in. Only the larger cities, however, are in any way as yet adequately supplied. No more admirable work has been undertaken than that among lepers, first initiated by John Newton in Ludhiana, Punjab (Presbyterian). Mr. W. C. Bailey, who had participated in this work, was instrumental in founding a society in London. The Gossner (German) Mission at Punelia conducts the largest work for lepers in India. Many other asylums have been established where the sufferers are tenderly cared for and led to the great physician. A most important phase is the separation of yet untainted children from leprous parents and the care of them in separate homes.

Temperance Work

This branch of reform is not exclusively a phase of Christian missions, as the Anglo-Indian Temperance Association stands at the head of the work and is supported by many distinguished Hindus. Mission work has, however, greatly impressed and extended temperance sentiment. In many missions, notably those of American Baptists in Assam and Burma, all converts promise total abstinence before baptism is administered. Native Hindus as well as Mohammedans are, as a rule, abstemious, and it is cause for profound regret that, in the twenty years from 1874 to 1894, under the excise laws of the British government, the revenue for sales of liquor nearly doubled.

The Student Volunteer Movement

All the world has felt the thrill of the fresh enthusiasm infused into the world's missions by the Student Volunteer Movement. Although the most recent of general missionary organizations, its roots reach back to the immortal "Haystack" meeting at Williams College in 1806, the birthplace of American Foreign Missions. A handful of students, met for an outdoor service, took refuge from a thunderstorm beneath a haystack, and then and there resolved to "*send the gospel to the heathen*," and took for their simple, manly motto, "We can do it if we will." A college society was formed; others resulted; some of the original movers died early and are almost forgotten. Hall and Newell, who became missionaries to India, united in writing a pamphlet entitled, "The Conversion of the World; a Plea for Six Hundred Millions." Dr. John Scudder saw a copy in a sick-room, read it, and offered himself as the first medical missionary to India. A boy named James B. Taylor caught the spark of Scudder's deep devotion, prepared himself to become a missionary, and while in Princeton College, aided by Peter Gulick, founded the Philadelphian Society, which remains to this day the centre of activity there. In 1877, at an intercollegiate Christian conference, the missionary propaganda was engrafted upon the general movement for the promotion of the Christian life in colleges, and the Student Volunteer Movement was born. Inspiration was caught from the spirit of heroic consecration of the mission band of Cambridge University, England. At Northfield, in the summer of 1886, a hundred men volunteered for foreign service within a single month. Over five thousand are now on the various fields or under pledge to go. From the first the Student Volunteers have evinced the strongest sympathy with medical work. In 1898 Douglass Thornton, a delegate to the Cleveland conference from England, stated that *the majority of the Student Volunteer body in England were studying medicine.*

New life blood has filled the veins of all Christendom from the glorious uprising of Student Volunteers, which was termed by Mr. Moody the greatest religious movement of the century. Its effect on India is powerful. In 1897, during the conferences held in that country, one hundred and twenty-seven student delegates pledged themselves to devote their whole lives to Christian work in India.

Modern Protestant missions in India were reborn with the new India which followed the Mutiny. In the year 1851 there were 15,000 communicants of Protestant churches in all

India. In 1891 there were 215,769. The census returns for 1901, only as yet partially published, have been secured from India for this volume and will be found in a table in the Appendix. They furnish reasonable ground for high hope and fresh resolution.

Geography of the Century's Work

In the earlier part of the century the work begun in the four commercial centres — Calcutta, Bombay, Madras, and Rangoon — and in Colombo centred in the three great presidencies, in lower Burma, and in the island of Ceylon. Later, Assam, Oudh, N. W. Provinces, and the Punjab were penetrated, and work was pushed north and east into Kashmir and Sindh, which remain, however, but meagrely cultivated. Meanwhile Mysore had been entered, and, in extreme South India, Travancore, Tinnevelly, Madura, etc., had become the most highly cultivated of all Indian mission fields, certain missions being reported as "fully occupied." In Ceylon one-tenth of the population is now Christian. It is conceded that North India is a more difficult field than South, owing, perhaps, to the greater hold of Mohammedanism in the former. In general the feudatory states have been scarcely touched. The Nizam's dominions (Haidarabad) are the chief stronghold of Islam in the Deccan, and they are notoriously inaccessible to missionaries. There remain yet enormous populations hardly reached in Central Provinces, in Rajputana (where there are but two missionaries to every million inhabitants), in Behar (one missionary to every four millions), and in Bhopal, with its two millions, but just opened. Among native races, the Karens of Burma bid fair soon to merit the term "Christianized." But as we study the map we are forced to see that Christianity has as yet only laid hold of the fringes of the mighty peninsula.

ILLUSTRATIVE SELECTIONS

Hymn

The Son of God goes forth to war,
A kingly crown to gain;
His blood-red banner streams afar:
Who follows in His train?
Who best can drink his cup of woe,
Triumphant over pain,
Who patient bears his cross below,
He follows in His train.

That martyr first, whose eagle eye
Could pierce beyond the grave;
Who saw his Master in the sky,
And called on Him to save;
Like Him, with pardon on His tongue,
In midst of mortal pain,
He prayed for them that did the wrong:
Who follows in his train?

A noble band, the chosen few,
On whom the Spirit came,
Twelve valiant saints, their hope they knew,
And mocked the torch of flame;
They met the tyrant's brandished steel,
The lion's gory mane,
They bowed their necks the stroke to feel:
Who follows in their train?

A noble army, men and boys,
The matron and the maid,
Around the throne of God rejoice,
In robes of light arrayed.
They climbed the steep ascent of heaven,
Through peril, toil, and pain;
O God, to us may grace be given
To follow in their train.

—R. Heber, Bishop of Calcutta 1822–1826.

"The Consecrated Cobbler"

Christian England laughed when Sydney Smith sneered at William Carey as a "consecrated cobbler," going on a fool's errand to convert the heathen. Carey died, aged seventy-three years. He was visited on his death-bed by the Bishop of India, the head of the Church of England in that land, who bowed his head and invoked the blessing of the dying missionary. The British authorities had denied to Carey a landing-place on his first arrival in Bengal; but when he died, the government dropped all its flags to half-mast in honor of a man who had done more for India than any of their generals. The universities of England, Germany, and America paid tribute to his learning, and to-day Protestant Christianity honors him as one of its noblest pioneers.

Hymn

O thou, my soul, forget no more
  The Friend who all thy sorrows bore.
Let every idol be forgot;
  But, O my soul, forget Him not.

Renounce thy works and ways, with grief,
  And fly to this divine relief;
Nor Him forget, who left His throne,
  And for thy life gave up His own.

Eternal truth and mercy shine
  In Him, and He Himself is thine:
And canst thou, then, with sin beset,
  Such charms, such matchless charms, forget?

O no: till life itself depart,
  His name shall cheer and warm my heart;
And, lisping this, from earth I'll rise,
  And join the chorus of the skies.

—Krishna Pal (first Hindu baptized by
Dr. Carey, 1800), translated by Marshman.

"India's Despised Apostles"

The anti-missionaries call them fools, madmen, tinkers, Calvinists, and schismatics, and keep out of sight their love of men and their zeal for God, and their self-devotedness, their indefatigable industry, their unequalled learning. These "low-born and low-bred mechanics" have translated the whole Bible into Bengali, and have by this time printed it. They are printing the New Testament in the Sanskrit, Orissa, Mahratta, the Hindustanee, the Guzerattee, and translated into Persic, Telinga, Carnata, Chinese, the language of the Sikhs and the Burmese. Extraordinary as this is, it will appear still more so when it is remembered that of these men one was originally a shoemaker, another a printer at Hull, and the third the master of a charity school at Bristol. Only fourteen years have elapsed since Thomas and Carey set foot in India, and in that time these missionaries have acquired this gift of tongues. In fourteen years these "low-born, low-bred mechanics" have done more to spread the knowledge of the Scriptures among the heathen than has been accomplished or even attempted by all the world beside.

—Robert Southey, in *Quarterly Review*, 1807.

Epitaph of Christian Frederic Schwartz (1798) on his tomb at Tanjore, written by the Rajah Serfojee, to whom he had acted as guardian:—

Firm wast thou, humble and wise,
Honest, pure, free from disguise,
Father of orphans, the widow's support,
Comfort in sorrow of every sort.
To the benighted, dispenser of light,
Doing, and pointing to that which is right.
Blessing to princes, to people, to me;
May I, my father, be worthy of thee!
Wisheth and prayeth thy Sarabojee.

My brethren, it were madness to shut our eyes to the fact that Christianity has come to India. It is not a passing episode; it is a mighty conquering and permanent spiritual power, come to stay and repeat its victories.

—*Brahman Lawyer.*

Preparatio Evangelica of the Serampore Triad

It is absolutely necessary :—

1. That we set an infinite value upon immortal souls.
2. That we gain all information of the snares and delusions in which these heathen are held.
3. That we abstain from all those things which would increase their prejudices against the gospel.
4. That we watch all opportunities for doing good.
5. That we keep to the example of Paul, and make the great subject of our teaching Christ the Crucified.
6. That the natives should have entire confidence in us, and feel quite at home in our company.
7. That we should build up and watch over the souls that may be gathered.
8. That we form our native brethren to usefulness, fostering every kind of genius, and cherishing every gift and grace in them, especially advising the native churches to choose their own pastors and deacons from amongst their own countrymen.
9. That we labor with all our might in forwarding translations of the Sacred Scriptures in the languages of India.
10. That we establish native free schools, and recommend these establishments to other Europeans.
11. That we be constant in prayer and the cultivation of personal religion to fit us for the discharge of these laborious and unutterably important labors. Let us often look at Brainerd in the woods of America pouring out his very soul before God for the perishing heathen, without whose salvation nothing could make him happy.

12. That we give ourselves unreservedly to this glorious cause. Let us never think that our time, our gifts, our strength, our families, or even the clothes we wear, are our own. Let us sanctify them all to God and His cause. O that He may sanctify us for His work! No private family ever enjoyed a greater portion of happiness than we have done since we resolved to have all things in common. If we are enabled to persevere, we may hope that multitudes of converted souls will have reason to bless God through all eternity for sending His gospel into this country.

The Apostle to Burma

It may be well to consider for a moment the *task* which Judson had set before him. What did they propose to do, this man of twenty-five and his young wife, standing amid the level rice-fields on the coast of lower Burma, with their faces turned landward toward towns and cities swarming with idolaters and hilltops crowded with heathen temples and pagodas? Their purpose was to undermine an ancient religion deeply fixed in the hearts and habits of four hundred millions of human beings. — Edward Judson.

In the Baptist meeting-house at Malden, Mass., is a marble tablet bearing the following inscription: —

IN MEMORIAM.
Rev. ADONIRAM JUDSON,
Born August 9, 1788.
Died April 12, 1850.
Malden his Birthplace.
The Ocean his Sepulchre.
Converted Burmans and
The Burman Bible
His Monument.
His Record is on High.

A Heathen Appeal

Hindus! awake, or you are lost. How many thousands have these missionaries turned to Christianity! On how many more have they cast their nets! If we sleep as heretofore, in a short time they will turn us all to Christianity, and our temples will be changed into churches. Is there no learned Pundit to be secured for money who will crush the Christians? . . . How long will water remain in a reservoir which continually lets out but receives none in? Let all the people join as one man to banish Christianity from the land. — *Recent Hindu (Tamil) Tract.*

The Empire of Love

Alexander, Cæsar, Charlemagne, and myself founded great empires; but upon what did the creations of our genius depend? Upon force. Jesus alone founded his empire upon love, and to this very day millions would die for Him. — *Words of Napoleon Bonaparte.*

Conversion of Brahmans

No higher evidence of human sincerity need be looked for than when a lordly Brahman consents to bend in penitential humility at the feet of a man as destitute of caste as is Chimman Lal, the native preacher, and entreats him to pour from his hand upon that proud head the water which forever breaks this Brahman's caste. When, in addition, this "aristocrat by creation" voluntarily and promptly takes off from his breast the emblem and outward sign of his nobility (the sacred thread), and hands it over with his string of praying beads to the administrator of the holy rite, he has done all that man can do in India to prove his earnestness and honesty.

On this occasion (at Ajudhiya, March, 1885) there were one hundred and twenty-seven of these Brahmans who did all this, and that, too, in public and before thousands of their own people, who had hitherto honored them as the clergy caste and nobility. — B. H. Badley.

Words of Witness

During the few months since I came home from India I have often had occasion to talk with men in high, powerful, and influential positions, and not seldom have I been asked with honest earnestness and great solicitude what ought, in my judgment, to be done for India. To this I have always answered, without reserve or hesitation, that, according to my view, *we should stand out in India as a Christian government.*

— Sir Herbert Edwardes, 1860.

Make him a Christian and make him a missionary.

— *Daily Prayer of Dr. John Scudder for his Son.*

No love in this dark world has ever seemed to me so much like the Saviour's as that of Dr. Newton for his lepers. — By One who knew him.

I feel my heart more and more engaged in the great work, and so much set upon it that I would rather undergo all the perils of a journey from Holland overland to Hindustan, should it be impracticable to obtain a passage by sea, than not go upon the glad errand.

— Carey to Andrew Fuller, 1793.

"Was not Dr. Carey once a shoemaker?" said a young British officer who had just met him at a social gathering in India. "No, sir," said Dr. Carey, quietly turning on the questioner, "only a cobbler."

Personally, I owe all that I have attained to the American missionaries, and no one can tell the incalculable good they have done to my people.

— NATIVE OF CEYLON.

Having studied the Vedas, the Koran, and the Tripitakas of the Buddhists, I have nowhere found a prayer so brief and all-comprehensive as that which the Christians call the Lord's Prayer.

— RAJAH RAMMOHUN ROY, 1822.

"No foreigner has ever entered the Punjab who has done so much for the Punjab as Padre Forman Sahib."

—*From a Lahore anti-Christian Newspaper*, 1894.

Would to God, my honored brethren, the time were arrived when not only in heart and hope, but visibly, we shall be one fold as well as under one shepherd. After all, why do we differ? Surely, the leading points which keep us asunder are capable of explanation or of softening.

—*Letter of Bishop Heber to the Serampore Triad*, June 3, 1824.

It is a part of a missionary's trials rightly to bear the impatience and contradictions, insolence and reproaches, of men who are sunk to the lowest degradation both mental and moral. — GORDON HALL, 1812–1826.

When asked in America what were the discouragements in the missionary work, Dr. John Scudder answered, "I do not know the word. I long ago erased it from my vocabulary."

THEMES FOR STUDY OR DISCUSSION

I. Christian Martyrs of India.
II. Schwartz, the Christian.
III. The Serampore Triad.
IV. William Wilberforce, Statesman and Philanthropist.
V. The Decade 1810–1820 in the History of Indian Missions. Great Men at Work. Great Organizations formed.
VI. Alexander Duff, the Founder of English Education in India.
VII. What did the Mutiny mean to the Missionary Enterprise?
VIII. England and the Opium Traffic and Excise Laws.
IX. Notable Native Christians (Men).
X. The Haystack Missionary Meeting and its Latest Outgrowth, the Student Volunteer Movement, both in England and America.
XI. To what Extent is Denominational Coöperation practicable in Indian Missions?
XII. Mass Movements in the Evangelization of India. (Karens, Kols, Telugus, Garos, South Indians.)

BOOKS OF REFERENCE

General Reference as before. In Addition:—

Report of Ecumenical Conference, 1900.
Reports of Student Volunteer Conferences, 1898, 1902.
Missionary Periodical Publications and Denominational Handbooks (especially for IX).
Clair-Tisdall's "India."
Biographies of Carey, Duff, Martyn, Wilson, by George Smith; of Heber, by Montefiore; of Judson, by Edward Judson; of Carey, Duff, Judson, and Martyn, in the Annals Series; of Butler, by Miss Butler.
Graham's "Missionary Expansion since the Reformation."

For particular reference on themes given above: —

Butler's "Land of the Veda," VII.
Carus-Wilson's "Life of Irene Petrie," X.
Clarke's "Study of Christian Missions," XI.
Mrs. Clough's "While sewing Sandals," IX, XII.
Dennis's "Christian Missions and Social Progress," VIII, IX, XII.
Dennis's "Foreign Missions after a Century," VIII, XI.
Downie's "History of the Telugu Mission," IX, XII.
Hodgkins's "Via Christi," I, II, III.
Holcomb's "Men of Might in India Missions," II, III, V, VI, X.
Lawrence's "Modern Missions in the East," VII, XII.
Leonard's "Missionary Annals of the Nineteenth Century," V, VII, X, XII.
Marshman's "Carey, Marshman, and Ward" (out of print), III, IV.
Mott's "Strategic Points in the World's Conquest," X.
Satthianadhan's "Sketches of India Christians," IX.
Sherring's "History of Protestant Mission in India," II, III, V, VI, XII.
Smith's "Conversion of India." For all but IV, VIII, X, XI.
Thoburn's "India and Malaysia," II, III, V, VI, IX, XII.
Thoburn's "Missionary Apprenticeship," VII.
Warneck's "Outline of History of Protestant Missions," II, III, V, VI, XII.

IMPORTANT DATES IN HISTORY OF WORK FOR THE WOMEN OF INDIA

1800–1807 Hannah Marshman establishes girls' schools.

1802 . . . Female infanticide forbidden by law.

1816 . . . Ann H. Judson teaches women and children of Burma.

1822 . . . Miss Cooke, C. M. S., opens schools for secluded women.

1825 . . . Wives of Bombay missionaries open schools.

1829 . . . Suttee abolished.

1834 . . . First English women's missionary society. F. E. S. (Church of England.)

1837 . . . Ladies' societies of Church of Scotland for female education in India.

1851 . . . First ladies' medical missionary society, Philadelphia, founded by Sarah J. Hale.

1856 . . . Remarriage Act passed.

1861 . . . Woman's Union Missionary Society founded by Mrs. Doremus.

1868–1878 Formation of women's societies in leading denominations of United States and Canada.

1869 . . . Dr. Clara Swain, first lady missionary physician, goes to Bareilly.

1876 . . . Indian universities open to women.

1880 . . . Dr. Fanny Butler, first English lady physician, goes to Kashmir.

1884 . . . Miss Chandra Mukhi Bose takes degree of M.A. at University of Calcutta.

1886 . . . Dr. Joshee takes medical degree.

1886 . . . Lady Dufferin Association.

1886 . . . Ramabai's first visit to America.

1886 . . . W. C. T. U. introduced into India.

1891 . . . Age of consent raised by law to twelve years.

1893 . . . Miss Cornelia Sorabji admitted to the bar at Bombay.

1894 . . . North India School of Medicine for Christian women.

CHAPTER V

A CENTURY OF WORK FOR WOMEN

> For Mercy has a human heart;
> Pity, a human face;
> And Love, the human form divine;
> And Peace, the human dress.
>
> —WILLIAM BLAKE.

THE hall-mark of modern Hinduism is the degradation of women. Woman is the "gate to hell," "a whirlpool of suspicion," "a dwelling-place of vices," "a poison that appears like nectar." Only to a mother of sons, and above all to a mother-in-law, is respect or consideration accorded.

I. SUMMARY OF WOMAN'S WRONGS

The chief of the social wrongs of woman are, in brief, her marriage in infancy to a man arbitrarily chosen for her, her possible child-widowhood, her entering into married life at ten or twelve years, the physical injuries of premature motherhood combined with neglect of all proper treatment, her absolute ignorance, her enforced and unnatural seclusion. To these must be added the nameless evils of polygamy and concubinage, the possible doom of infanticide not yet wholly done away with, and the low moral tone of family life.

Without further recapitulation we will quote Mr. Kipling's verdict, and proceed to consider what has thus far been accomplished by various agencies toward the uplifting of the status of Indian women and the mitigation of their sufferings.

Verdict of a Close Observer

"The matter with this country," says Mr. Kipling, than whom no man knows his India better, "is not in the least political, but an all-round entanglement of physical, social, and moral evils and corruption, all more or less due to the unnatural treatment of women. You cannot gather figs from thistles, and so long as the system of infant marriage, the prohibition of the remarriage of widows, the lifelong imprisonment of wives in a worse than penal confinement, and the withholding from them of any kind of education as rational beings continues, the country cannot advance a step. Half of it is morally dead, and worse than dead, and that is just the half from which we have a right to look for the best impulses. The foundations of life are rotten, utterly rotten, and beastly rotten. The men talk of their rights and privileges. I have seen the women that bear these men. May God forgive the men!"

II. GOVERNMENT REFORMS

Female Infanticide

In 1794, within the year after his arrival in India, Carey discovered the practice of sacrificial infanticide at the annual festivals at Ganga Sagar and on the Ganges. Through his friend, Mr. Udny, the atrocious crime was laid before Lord Wellesley, then governor-general, and a statesman of humane and enlightened views. Mr. Carey's position as Professor of Bengali in Fort William College at Calcutta, surrounded by learned pundits from all parts of the empire, gave him peculiar advantages in investigating the subject, and he was appointed by government to report upon it. His labors were successful. A law was speedily passed prohibiting this form of human sacrifice under severe penalty. From that time open infanticide has ceased; but the death-rate among girl babies continues to be singularly excessive. The census of 1870 revealed "the curious fact" that three hundred female infants were stolen *by wolves* from within the city of Amritsar.

Suttee

From the period of his settlement in Serampore Carey had been unremitting in his endeavors to draw the attention of government to the practice of suttee, having been roused to a passion of indignation by witnessing the burning of a shrieking, struggling woman held forcibly down to the pile. This custom was not enjoined by the Code of Manu, and was therefore a later enactment of the Brahmans, for what purpose or with what motive has never been fully determined. The motive of the victim, who thus immolated herself on the funeral pyre of her husband, is not far to seek. She was assured of a glorious and immediate entrance into paradise by this voluntary death; if she avoided it, she was assured of the wretched ignominy of despised widowhood. Carey and his colleagues, in 1804, sent ten agents from village to village within a circuit of thirty miles of Calcutta, to collect information regarding the practice. They reported that within those villages more than three hundred widows had been burned within six months. He further learned from the pundits that suttee was "simply encouraged as a virtue" by the Shastras, not commanded.

Carey embodied all the results of his investigation in a memorial which he presented to Lord Wellesley. *This was the first official notice regarding suttee ever placed on the government records.* Lord Wellesley, who was inclined personally to a prohibitory act, unhappily left his seat of office seven days later. A reactionary policy, actuated by anti-liberal and anti-missionary prejudice, followed; all hope of prompt and vigorous action vanished, and during the following twenty-five years seventy thousand widows ascended the pile and met their fiery death, while Carey "waited and prayed, and every day saw the devilish smoke ascend along the banks of the Ganges." In 1829, under the broad and benevolent rule of Lord Bentinck, an act was passed prohibiting suttee under stringent penal enactment.

It was not until 1856 that, after much agitation, an act was passed legalizing the remarriage of widows. In the forty-six years since that time only five hundred widows have remarried. The intensity of Hindu prejudice against such marriages, the despotic tyranny of custom, leads to persecution and obloquy which few men and women can face. In spite of the ardent efforts of Keshub Chunder Sen and other native reformers, the law thus far remains a dead letter.

Child Marriage

In 1871, Mr. Sen, as president of the Indian Reform Association, agitated the subject of raising the age for the consummation of marriage to fourteen years. His efforts were ably seconded by the Parsi reformer, Malabari, and also by the W. C. T. U. of Bombay. The horrible death of Phulmani Dasi, a little girl under twelve, in 1890, roused both the Indian and British public. Mrs. Monelle Mansell, an American medical missionary residing in Lucknow, framed a memorial to government signed by fifty-five lady physicians in India, citing facts coming under their own personal observation.

"These cases," says the *Indian Witness* of October, 1890, "are too horrible and sickening in their awful details to be given to the public. They prove *to the hilt* all the heavy charges brought against the system of child-marriage on the ground of suffering inflicted. Death, crippling for life, agony indescribable, torture that would put a fiend to shame — these are all here. If the officials of the Indian government can read this memorial without blenching, their hearts are turned to stone."

The memorial concludes: "In view of the above facts, the undersigned lady doctors and medical practitioners appeal to your Excellency's compassion to enact or introduce a measure by which the consummation of marriage will not be permitted before the wife has passed the full age of fourteen years."

Another memorial, to the same effect, addressed directly to her Majesty, the Queen Empress, was sent in, signed by eighteen hundred native ladies from all over India. Petitions and protests against such enactment were presented in force; but after thorough sifting, on March 19, 1891, a compromise measure was carried, and a bill was passed whereby the age of consent was raised from ten to twelve.

Similar reform measures, although in many

cases the age named is eight years, have been introduced into the feudatory states.

Education

In educational matters the government has followed a liberal policy for women. Besides the various schools of all grades open to girls, the five great Indian universities, at Madras, Bombay, Calcutta, Lahore, and Allahabad, are all open to women. Beginning in the year 1866, Mary Carpenter, an eminent Englishwoman, visited India four times with a view to improving the condition of the women, and at her instance several schools for them were founded by the British government.

For a number of minor government enactments in favor of women, we refer the student to Mrs. Fuller's invaluable book, "The Wrongs of Indian Womanhood."

The formula of the triologue of the British government, the oath administered in the Punjab by Lord Lawrence, partially epitomizes the reforms thus far undertaken: —

1. Thou shalt not burn thy widows.
2. Thou shalt not kill thy daughters.
3. Thou shalt not bury alive thy lepers.

III. THE WORK OF CHRISTIAN WOMEN

Early Laborers

The first direct effort made in behalf of the native women of India by a Christian woman was embodied in the day schools at Serampore opened by Mrs. Hannah Marshman in 1800 and 1807.

Among her pupils were Eurasian girls, a class met with all over India, the offspring of Europeans and natives. The Eurasians are a distinct element in the population, usually speaking English, and more easily accessible than full-blooded Hindus, as they are without caste. They are sometimes unfairly said to embody the vices of both races with the virtues of neither. The part of Eurasians in carrying the gospel to their sisters in the early days of the last century should never be forgotten. In 1819 a company of young Eurasians, who had been instructed by Mrs. Marshman, formed a society for the education of Indian women. In three years they had six schools and one hundred and sixty pupils.

About this time we read of Mrs. Judson's labors among the Burmese women, and of similar work by the wives of the Bombay missionaries, Mrs. Wilson in 1830 being reported as carrying on six schools. In 1821 Miss Cooke of the C. M. S., the first single woman to enter India as a missionary, began work among the Zenana women.

Beginnings

With the formation of the English Society for the Promoting Female Education in the

East — the F. E. S.— in 1834, and the Ladies' Societies of the Church of Scotland three years later, began the organized work of the Christian women of Great Britain for the women of India. In the United States, Women's Societies for the Promotion of Missionary Endeavor had existed even as early as 1800, when we hear of the Boston Female Society for promoting the Diffusion of Christian Knowledge. Similar societies came into existence in all the larger denominations in the first half of the century, and in 1851 a Ladies' Medical Missionary Society was formed in Philadelphia by Mrs. S. J. Hale. It was not until 1861, however, that American women began to organize for the clearly defined purpose of supplementing general missionary work by sending unmarried women to work among the girls and women of heathen peoples, who could be reached only by women.

Mrs. T. C. Doremus of New York was the moving spirit in the earliest effort of this kind, viz., the Woman's Union Missionary Society, in which six different denominations were represented. Twenty-five years earlier Mrs. Doremus had been powerfully affected by the urgent appeal of David Abeel, an American missionary from China, through whose means the English F. E. S. had been established, and whose influence, thus extended to American women, has been world wide in its working.

o

The loving heart, the generous hand, and catholic spirit of Mrs. Doremus well typified the earnestness and enthusiasm of this early expression of missionary zeal. The first messengers direct from the Christian women of America to the women of India — Miss Marston, Miss Higby, and Miss Févré — were sent by the new society to Burma. In 1862 Miss Brittan was sent to Calcutta as a teacher in the zenanas, a word which had not until this time became familiar to American ears. Her work is known in Calcutta as the American Doremus Zenana Mission. Miss Brittan was later joined by a large force of workers, and the efforts of the society have extended to Allahabad, Rajpore, and other centres. The Union Society is not an auxiliary, but an independent and interdenominational organization.

English Societies

In England the formation of women's auxiliaries to the various missionary societies began somewhat earlier than in this country. In 1858 the women of the Wesleyan Methodist body formed a society in response to appeals of the wives of missionaries in India, and they now support about forty missionaries in the Madras and Calcutta presidencies and in Ceylon. In 1865 a society of ladies was formed in London, auxiliary to the S. P. G., which now sustains a very strong work in the Punjab. The English

Baptist Zenana Mission was instituted in 1867, and supports twenty missionaries in India at stations stretching from Calcutta to Madras. In 1880 was formed the Church of England Zenana Missionary Society, which is carrying on finely organized and vigorous work on evangelistic, educational, and medical lines.

First American Auxiliary

The first of the series of denominational auxiliaries to be organized in the United States was that of the Congregational women in Boston and vicinity, in the Old South Chapel in January, 1866. This meeting inspires peculiar interest as marking the rise of the great organized Woman's Work for Woman, which grew and spread with such effectual power and energy during the last quarter of the nineteenth century.

Mrs. Winslow, of the Madura Mission of the American Board, and Mrs. Butler, of the Methodist Mission in North India, were present. It was shown that the condition of women in India had always interposed an insuperable obstacle to the spread of the gospel; while many encouraging facts were given to prove that an effectual door was open for their evangelization by the plan proposed of sending out single women to labor for their own sex. Mrs. Butler showed clearly that the only means of reaching the secluded women then existing was through the wives of missionaries, who with their own family cares were wholly unequal to the work. Several single women had already offered themselves for the service. The hour was full of solemnity; an especial sense of the enduement of the Holy Spirit, with a new baptism of missionary consecration, rested upon the company. An organization was effected with the following as the first article of its constitution: —

"The object of this society is to engage the earnest, systematic coöperation of the women of New England with the existing boards for foreign missions in sending out and supporting unmarried female missionaries and teachers to heathen women." "It was a day of beginnings. Not one missionary in the field, not an auxiliary society to rest upon, only a few women full of faith and zeal — only these, and God. . . . In the incipient stage of the enterprise the membership knew not whereunto it was called; and a few months sufficed, by the great enlargement of the work, to show that it would be wiser for the ladies of each denomination to coöperate separately with their own foreign missionary board."

Shortly after, the words limiting the constituency of the society to New England were stricken from the name and constitution, and in March, 1869, the Woman's Board of Missions was incorporated, auxiliary to the A. B. C. F. M. The first number of the magazine, *Life and*

Light for Heathen Women, was issued during the same month.

A Decade of Organization

The decade 1868–1878 witnessed the formation of some kindred organization in almost every evangelical body of the United States and Canada, springing from this same root. In 1868 the Woman's Board of the Interior (Congregational) was formed, with its centre in Chicago.

In the chapel of the Tremont Street Methodist Church, Boston, on the 23d of March, 1869, Mrs. Butler, the wife of the founder of the India Mission, who had taken a deep interest in the formation of the Woman's Board, with Mrs. E. W. Parker, just returned from India, and six other ladies, organized the Woman's Foreign Missionary Society of the Methodist Church. At a meeting held a few weeks later the name of Isabella Thoburn was presented to the new society as ready to sail for India under their auspices, if appointed. Some timid ones shrank from so soon assuming the responsibility of a missionary's support, but Mrs. Edward F. Porter rose and exclaimed: "Shall we lose her because we have not the needed money in our hands? No, rather let us walk the streets of Boston in calico and save the expense of more costly apparel. Mrs. President, I move the appointment of Miss Thoburn as our missionary to India." The response of the meeting was unanimous, "We will send her." Vigorous Methodist societies have been formed since the first, both in the United States and in Canada, the latter not until 1881.

In 1870 the organization already existing for home missionary purposes among the Presbyterian women of New York enlarged its field of labor and adopted the name, the Ladies' Board of Missions of the Presbyterian Church, auxiliary to the home and foreign boards, and that same year were organized similar societies among Presbyterian women of Philadelphia and of the Northwest.

In 1871 the woman's auxiliary of the Foreign Missionary Society of the Protestant Episcopal Church was formed; and in the same year eleven Baptist ladies met in Newton Centre, Mass., "for the purpose of forming a woman's missionary society for the benefit of women in heathen lands." The appeals which led directly to this organization were contained in letters written in 1869 and 1870 by Mrs. Carpenter of Bassein, Burma. The girls' school was growing beyond the capacity of the busy, burdened missionary's wife, with her one helper, to meet. Mrs. Carpenter made a fervent appeal for "a woman of character and piety to take charge of the female department in the school. We are doing all we have strength for, but we see the harvest perishing for lack of reapers. Pray for us. *I am not sure that you yourselves have not a work to do for missions at home — the forming of women's societies auxiliary to the Missionary Union. I believe that is the true course.*" The Women's Society of the West (Baptist) was formed the same year.

Two years later the women of the Free-will Baptist body, who had maintained a society for circulating missionary intelligence and collecting funds since 1847, decided to take advanced ground, and with the approval of their Foreign Missionary Board to select and support thenceforth their own missionaries.

The Christian Woman's Board of Missions was organized in Cincinnati in October, 1874. For some years its work was largely confined to Jamaica, but in 1882 Miss Greybiel of New York with three other young women were sent to Ellichpore, India, as Bible teachers and missionaries. Though employed by the society, these all, at their own request, went out without stipulated salary, trusting to God and their sisters for support.

The Woman's Board of Foreign Missions of the Dutch Reformed Church began its work in 1875 in New York City, with Mrs. Jonathan Sturges as president. This church, "founded by the martyrs amid the fires of the Reformation in Holland," has carried on the famous Arcot Mission in India with characteristic thoroughness and devotion on the part of both men and women workers.

In September and October, 1876, the Baptist women of Canada, East and West, the former in Montreal, and the latter in Toronto, effected their organization for work in foreign missions. The Presbyterian Woman's Society of Canada followed the next year. Just over the line of the decade, in 1879, occurred the organization of the Lutheran Woman's Society. All these societies have entered with energetic life into the work of their respective boards in India.

Women's Work in India Demanded

Such, in brief, is the story of a decade of organized work of Christian women for their heathen sisters. It is impossible in this volume to describe the fields of labor or to name the noble women sent out to represent the societies. The ranks are constantly recruited by new organizations. The latest, but one of the most promising auxiliaries, is that of the Swedish Lutheran women, the K. M. A. of Stockholm. They began work in 1896 in Central Provinces. The work of all is done in perfect harmony with that of the affiliated boards, and it has proved an invaluable supplement to their enterprise. The necessity for this definite effort is so manifest that explanation and apology are wholly superfluous. Take Mr. Kipling's awful arraignment of the condition of Indian women, and place beside it the well-known impossibility of men missionaries reaching them, and there is but one solution to the problem, viz., the interposition of Christian women. To make such interposition most thorough and effective, separate but auxiliary organization is needful. All criticism of women's work as leading to diversion of gifts from the general treasury, and of needless multiplying of organizations, falls before the incontrovertible facts that the churches with the most active women's circles are uniformly the most generous contributors to general boards, and that the increase in knowledge of missionary interests is almost wholly dependent upon the efforts of women's societies. Thirty-five years ago there was not a woman's foreign missionary society in America; now there are 45 societies, more than 20,000 local auxiliaries, and 7000 mission bands. In 1899 there were 150,000,000 of printed pages sent out for use among this force of workers.

Seventy years ago Alexander Duff, studying the seclusion and degradation of women in Calcutta, said, that "to try to educate women in India was as vain as to attempt to scale a wall five hundred yards high." Dr. Duff, great as was his wisdom, was not prophet enough to see that in the last quarter of the nineteenth century a great army of women of holy heart and life would invade India, and prove mighty through God, not to scale that wall, but to throw it down. It is they, and they alone, who can reach the women of India.

IV. THREEFOLD METHOD OF CHRISTIAN WOMEN —EVANGELISTIC, EDUCATIONAL, MEDICAL

(1) Evangelistic.

The earliest method of evangelizing higher caste women was known as zenana work, meaning personal visits of missionaries to the secluded inmates of Hindu and Mohammedan homes. Precisely when this work was initiated, or by whom, cannot be determined; but it is certain that in 1840 Dr. T. Smith and Mr. and Mrs. Fordyce, of the Free Church of Scotland, began such a movement, and that such work was ably carried on also by Mrs. Mullens and Mrs. Sale. To the latter, wife of Rev. John Sale, missionary in Calcutta, is often given the credit of first entering the Hindu zenana with the message of salvation. The Baptist Zenana Missionary Society was an outgrowth of her work, followed by that of Mrs. Lewis. A slightly different method, also known as zenana work, was begun as early as 1822, by Miss Cooke of the C. M. S. This was largely educational, and the late Dowager Lady Kinnaird, through whose influence the Church of England Zenana Missionary Society (C. E. Z. M. S.) was formed, may be regarded as its mainstay. The Indian Female Normal School and Instruction Society was organized in 1852 for work among zenana women.

Aside from all educational efforts connected with it the work in zenanas has been, since the days of Mrs. Sale and Mrs. Mullens, the favorite channel of direct evangelization. In this close, heart-to-heart encounter the Christian missionary learns the needs and the sorrows of India's oppressed wives and mothers. Here, in the very deepest part of it, absolutely closed to men missionaries, the family life in all its multiform misery can be reached with the healing and purifying touch of Christianity. Empty-headed, frivolous, lifeless as is the ordinary Hindu or Mohammedan woman, she is yet within reach of the motives which the missionary thus brings to bear upon her, and great have been the results in leading such as these to Christ. There are now estimated to be fifty thousand zenanas in India open to the visits of Christian missionary women, but there are forty millions of women in zenanas who can be reached by no other agency.

Closely allied to this line of work is that of house-to-house visiting among non-secluded low-caste and non-caste women. This work devolves largely upon the single women sent out by our societies, as does also the work of training those most invaluable adjuncts to their work, the native Biblewomen, whose knowledge of the mental and social habits of their country-women enables them to reach their real needs as it is hardly possible for English and American women to do. High faith and courage have been shown by these native helpers, who, in the testing times of plague and famine, have proved themselves made of heroic stuff. In addition to their common routine, the Biblewomen often visit the great heathen festivals, and engage in personal work among the deluded worshippers of Jagan-nath and Krishna, with a good measure of success. An effective method is that of "touring," travelling from village to village in a house-boat, or with a tent, everywhere speaking to the women of Christ's salvation, and distributing tracts and Bibles. The instruction of the women of the native church in the rudiments of Christian doctrine is another important branch of women's work.

(2) **Educational.**

The evangelistic work of women missionaries, since it does not include public preaching, is of necessity closely allied to teaching, not only exclusively religious teaching in Bible schools, but general teaching in boarding and day schools, for Hindus and Mohammedans alike, where the basis of a secular and religious education is laid at the same time.

This school work is of paramount importance, and as the most diligent care is given that the secular side does not overshadow the religious, the Christian schools are the seed beds of the native church. Here are received, from childhood to maturity, the vitalizing germs of Christian truth; and forth from these almost innumerable schools are going by hundreds the Christian young men and women who are the hope of India. The effectual principle of the Roman Church to secure the training of children in their earliest years, thus stamping its influence upon them in the most impressible period, has been wisely adopted by Protestant missionaries. Great stress is now laid upon Christian primary schools and kindergartens, and with notable results.

Excellent high schools for girls under missionary management are scattered throughout the country, some of which may speedily develop into full-course colleges. Others of marked usefulness, as the English Baptist school in Delhi, oblige the girls to learn the use of grain fans and millstones, or spinning, weaving, laundry work, needlework, embroidery, and many other useful crafts.

In 1896 there were in the Madras presidency over 1000 schools, attended by about 110,000 girls. Similar figures can be given for other parts of India. A transformation is being accomplished which centuries of merely human wisdom could not have wrought. The time will soon have wholly gone by when a girl to be *respectable* must be married at ten or twelve.

And yet there is even now in India but one woman missionary for every 160,000 of the native women.

Women's Colleges

There are two Christian colleges for women, the earliest founded being Lucknow College in North India, an institution of the American Methodist Mission; and the Sarah Tucker College in Palamcotta, South India, under the C. M. S. The former receives all pupils sent, without regard to race or language, and has combined in one happy family, Hindustani, Bengali, English, and Eurasian girls, all trained to work for Christ. This school is affiliated with Allahabad University, and Palamcotta College with the Madras University.

The fact that the government colleges are open to women has been mentioned. A large majority of the young women who have entered these universities are Christians. The first candidate was Miss Chandra Mukhi Bose, who was prepared in the American Presbyterian Mission at Dehra Dun, and passed her entrance examination in 1876. She won her degree and is dean of the Bethune Girls' College (government) at Calcutta. In this institution all the pupils, as it happens, are Hindu, none Mohammedan. The Mohammedan youth of both sexes are persistently slow in responding to intellectual appeal.

Since the universities were opened to women, from 1870 to 1899, 1306 women have passed the entrance examination. Of these about

367 are native Christians; 27 Hindus, 1 Mohammedan, 728 European or Eurasian; the rest are divided between other nationalities.

One of the most impressive addresses of the Ecumenical Conference of 1900 was that of Miss Lilavati Singh, B.A., a young Hindu lady, professor of English literature at Lucknow College. So intense was Miss Singh's eagerness to acquire English, that while in school she read Green's History of England through seven times. After hearing her address on the "Results of Higher Education," the late ex-President Harrison remarked, "*If I had given a million dollars to foreign missions, I should count it wisely invested if it led only to the conversion of that one woman.*"

Efforts of Native Christian Women

The conspicuous educational and philanthropic labors of the Parsi family, Mrs. Sorabji and her daughters, and of the whole world's heroine, the Pundita Ramabai, must be briefly mentioned. There is no connection between the two movements, although all their schools are in Poona, and the workers are in warm sympathy with each other.

Twenty-five years ago Mrs. Sorabji, the wife of one of the first converts to Christianity from among the Parsis, founded in that "Stronghold of Brahmanism," Poona, a hundred miles southeast of Bombay, several vernacular and Anglo vernacular schools for the children of English, Parsis, Mohammedans, and Hindus. Mrs. Sorabji has also established, with the aid of her daughters (one of whom is the first native woman of India to take the degree of Doctor of Civil Laws), the Victoria High School, which has received the most cordial commendation of the Duke of Connaught, the Bishop of Bombay, and others in high station. These schools furnish not only admirable mental training, according to the best European methods, but the Bible is diligently taught, and the teaching throughout is vitalized by a spirit of devout Christian love.

The reports of these schools are full of suggestions of peculiar interest, and cast much light on the relative ability and varying characteristics of Mohammedan, Hindu, and Parsi children.

Other efforts of native women for their sisters, such as that of Miss Chakarbulty of Allahabad, and of the "Daughters of India," if less striking than those of the gifted Sorabji family, are full of profound interest and brightest promise for the future.

Pundita Ramabai

Probably no one will dispute the assertion that Ramabai is the most distinguished woman in India to-day, whether foreign or native.

Born in 1858, in Gungamal, in the western Ghats of India, of Brahman parents, Ramabai was carefully educated by her father, a man of remarkably advanced views, learning not only many dialects, but gaining a thorough knowledge of Sanskrit. Her intellectual attainment was such that in 1877 the highest title possible for a native woman was conferred upon her by the pundits of Calcutta, "Sarasvati, Goddess of Wisdom." Coming into contact with the famous Hindu reformer, Keshub Chunder Sen, Ramabai's faith in idolatry was shaken, and a dim consciousness of her relation to God dawned upon her. After her husband's death, being deeply moved for the cruel sufferings of child-wives and child-widows, Ramabai consecrated herself to work for their emancipation from their awful bondage.

Going to England in 1883 to seek such training as she felt necessary for the successful prosecution of this work, the Pundita was soon brought into the clear light of Christian faith. Her first visit to America, where she travelled the length and breadth of the land, telling the impassioned story of her sisters' wrongs, led to the formation, May 28, 1887, of the Ramabai Association, pledged to support for ten years a school for high-caste Hindu widows. That night she was found sobbing in her room and exclaimed, "I am crying for joy that my dream of years has become a reality."

In 1889 her school in Bombay, soon removed to Poona, was opened with two pupils. It was named Sharada Sadan (Home of Wisdom) and is secular. In 1897 Ramabai visited the famine district and rescued 300 high-caste girls from sin and death. The school she opened for them is known as "Mukti" (Salvation) and is frankly Christian, as is a third school called Kripa Sadan (Home of Grace). In all three Ramabai now cares for 2000 of these suffering child-widows.

There are 27,000,000 widows in India today; 281,000 of them are under fifteen years of age; 14,000 are less than four. Of their grievous lot we have read in an earlier chapter. "Ask Christian women," said Ramabai, fourteen years ago, "to help me educate these child-widows, for I solemnly believe that this hated and despised class of women, educated and enlightened, are by God's grace to redeem India."

"*Seeing Ramabai's great love*," said one under her charge, in explaining how she had been led to Christ. This impassioned, motherlike, Christlike love is the secret of Ramabai's marvellous success.

"I was overwhelmed," said Dr. Klopsch, after a visit to the schools at Poona, "by the magnitude and quality of the work carried on with a success that is almost incredible. Pundita Ramabai is surely one of God's chosen ones, divinely called to her mission."

It should be borne in mind that the mighty systems of paganism in India, whether Hindu, Buddhistic, or Mohammedan, are alike destitute of all those fruits of Christianity which we term charitable, philanthropic, benevolent. Where are the hospitals, dispensaries, orphanages, asylums for the leper, the blind, the deaf and mute? They have no place in the heathen economy. For this reason there is a peculiar significance in such a movement as that of Ramabai, suggesting the mighty power for its own healing and renovation which resides in *native India*, when once it becomes energized by the master-motive of Christian love.

(3) **Medical.**

The first qualified woman physician who ever entered Asia to practise her profession was Miss Clara Swain, of Castile, N. Y., who was sent out in 1869 by the American Methodist Woman's Foreign Missionary Society. Miss Swain settled at Bareilly, and began her work without delay with characteristic energy, treating in the first six weeks after her arrival 108 patients, while during the first year 1225 patients were prescribed for at the mission house, and in 1874 the number reached 3000. Early in her residence in Bareilly a native gentleman, who called her to attend his wife, welcomed her with these words: "We need lady physicians in India very much, and I have often spoken of it to my friends; but we did not know where to look for them, as our women are uneducated, and could not study medicine. But light has again dawned upon us from America."

In less than three months after her arrival Miss Swain formed a class of sixteen native educated girls in the study of medicine. Three years later thirteen members passed their final examination in the presence of two civil surgeons, and were granted certificates of practice in all ordinary diseases.

Dr. Swain carried the gospel with her in all her work, the Bible being read and religious instruction habitually given in her zenana visits, and thus entrance was gained to many homes hitherto closed against missionary effort. The comment of a Hindu woman to another lady physician embodies the point of view of many: "Your God must be a very kind, good God to send a doctor to the women. None of our gods ever sent us a doctor."

In brief time Dr. Swain felt the need of an adequate dispensary and a hospital for women. The Nawab of Rampore freely gave an estate in Bareilly valued at fifteen thousand dollars for the purpose. Both buildings were erected in 1872 and 1873, at a cost of over ten thousand dollars, which was borne by the Methodist Woman's Society at home. The plan of the hospital is similar to that of an eastern hotel. On a slight elevation stand the buildings, with two rows of dormitories, verandas extending the whole length of each. The grounds are tastefully laid out, and made beautiful with tropical shrubbery. The dispensary is opened at six o'clock every morning except Sunday. Dispensary cards are printed in three different characters, — Hindi, Parsi, and Urdu. Each card has a verse of Scripture printed on the back. It may happen that a score of different castes and half a dozen religions will be represented in the consulting room in a few months. Bible women work among the patients while they wait their turn.

We have briefly recapitulated the essential features of the activity of the first American lady physician and described the first woman's hospital in India, because they are typical and include the main features of all the medical missionary work now conducted by nearly every Woman's Board which has followed. In all we find the welcome to the "Doctor Miss Sahib," on the part of natives, high or low; the well-equipped dispensary and hospital; the practice in these and in the home, with the strong admixture of religious teaching; the open door to the zenana, which is firmly closed to the male missionaries, whether evangelist or physician; the training of native women in nursing, hygiene, and the practice of medicine. To these may be added, as the terrible exigencies of the late years of plague and famine have called for them, relief and diet kitchens, and sanitary committee inspection, most important in Indian villages, where wells and ponds are used alike for bathing, washing of clothing, and drinking, and where utter neglect of the common laws of cleanliness breeds disease on every hand. The barbarous native practice of midwifery, the inconceivable suffering of the native women through the violation of all the laws of their physical life, and the iron bonds of superstition laid on all alike, increase the need of enlightened medical practice, while they add a hundred-fold to the obstacles in its way.

From an article by Dr. Joyce, of the London Missionary Society, we quote : —

"Childbirth brings pollution for a certain term of days to an Indian woman. Instead of the love and gentle tendance and skilful nursing that are given among us to a woman in her hour of need, the Indian mother is regarded for the time being as unclean and unapproachable by the members of her family. No one except a servant or native midwife is allowed to attend her. A matted-in portion of the veranda, a lumber-room, a cowshed, or a coalshed are too often regarded as more than sufficient and suitable shelter for the young mother. Everything she touches is rendered unclean, so the scantiest allowance of necessaries is given to her. Often in a state of appalling insanitation, without proper attendance, denied the entrance of air and light, unwashed, neglected, ill fed and sometimes unfed, the young mothers, often themselves mere children in age, pass through their time of trial. Many succumb, some emerge, apparently unhurt, too many endure for differing periods of years, sometimes for life, suffering engendered by want of care and love and skill that should have been lavished so freely."

A phase of work common among our medical missionaries is itinerary practice ; the journeying from village to village with well-filled medicine cases, clinics morning, noon, and night, and the gospel given all the time. Dr. Pauline Root recounts one of her tours, when she often treated eighty patients before breakfast and two hundred and fifty in a day, as a whole village would stream out to her little tent, bearing their sick folk to lay before her, while she herself had not time so much as to eat.

Truly it is a programme of power immeasurable and of toil unspeakable but full of glory. It is a Christlike thing. Perhaps if Protestants canonized their noblest souls, we should have for a saint Mary Reed, the American Methodist missionary in Cawnpore, who, in 1890, discovered that she was herself a leper, and thereupon deciding to give what might be left of life to work among lepers, withdrew into the foothills of the Himalayas to a colony of these smitten outcasts, where to-day she is living in cheerful, self-effacing ministration.

A Typical Medical Missionary

We give below a description written very recently of a Woman's Board medical missionary now in West India, a graduate of Wellesley College in 1886, not because we believe it to be exceptional but typical, not ideal but real:—

"We who live with her cannot adequately express our reverence and gratitude for her — she is so sympathetic, so self-denying, so skilful, *so Christian.* Many are the lives which she has saved. I should like to have people in America see, as I have done, this cultured college lady down on her knees on a dirty, earthen floor, in a room full of smoke and discomfort, putting her arms around a dirty man with blood flowing from his mouth and nose, lifting him into a more comfortable position, and applying ice and water to the head and neck to stop the flow. Not long ago she spent seven nights out of eight in a native house caring for a woman who had been given up for dead, and for whose funeral people had begun to make preparations, and she succeeded in bringing her back to health. That woman is now a healthy woman in an important home.

"If one ever visits her dispensary, it is amazing to see the crowd that is waiting for her ministration. Good-caste women, low-caste women, educated women, ignorant women, all kinds of children, and outside even many men hoping that after the women and children have gone they may get some attention."

Of another the following incident is told: "One day, while the name of the patient was being written down in the register, a hand was stretched out and put lovingly on the writer's, and a voice said gently, '*Mem* Sahib, you are like the Lord Jesus.' The question was put, 'Why do you say so?' Pointing to the curtain which divides the veranda from the dispensary, she replied, 'Out there have I not heard that Jesus healed the sick, went about preaching in the villages, and said kind words to women?' There was no denying the fact. 'Well, you do all that, so you are like Him.'"

The increase in woman's medical missionary work can be noted by the report of the dispensary practice of Dr. Julia Bissell at Ahmednagar for 1901, which extended to 31,160 patients.

It is impossible here to recount the steps by which the movement has grown, but at the present time each auxiliary, whether English, Scotch, Canadian, or American, has its *medical arm*, its own hospitals, and its own staff of women practitioners. Never was a more inspiring field of labor open to Christian young women physicians than India offers to-day. Let it be remembered that male physicians are wholly debarred from attendance on the high-caste women, who would rather die than be seen and cared for by them.

And for all the millions of suffering women in India there are but eighty-five women medical missionaries now at work in the field. Of these forty-six are English. Although medical missions were begun in India by American, they have been taken up with more enthusiasm by English societies, who, in 1880, sent out the first medical missionary of the C. E. Z. M. S., Dr. Fanny Butler, whose life and work for nine years in North India and Kashmir have made her name one which can never be forgotten.

The Countess of Dufferin Fund

For many years missionaries carried on the medical work for women in India alone; but in 1885 an incident occurred which has resulted in a great secular movement in England in this direction under royal patronage. We will leave the romantic story of the English missionary, Miss Bielby, her patient, the Maharani of Poona, and her locket with its heart-rending message to the Queen of England, for a special theme of study. Suffice it to say that the message went straight to the Queen's compassionate heart, and in consequence Lady Dufferin, wife of the viceroy-elect, who was just sailing for

India, was commissioned by her Majesty to do all within her power to relieve the suffering women of India. Wise and prompt in her measures, Lady Dufferin soon established an organization known as the National Association for supplying Female Medical Aid to the Women of India, its stated objects being: medical tuition, medical relief, and the supply of trained midwives and nurses for women and children. A million or more women are treated annually, directly or indirectly, by means of this powerful agency.

Mrs. Claxton, who has been president of the Woman's Baptist Foreign Missionary Society of eastern Ontario since its inception, is in receipt of a personal letter from Lady Dufferin, written during her residence in India, explicitly defining the aims and scope of this organization.

"The particular need for medical help for women in this country," writes Lady Dufferin, "is, from the very nature of the subject, one upon which it is difficult to write. There can be no doubt that marrying extremely young, that living a life of extreme seclusion, that being often victims of superstitious practices and of grossly ignorant treatment, the women of India must suffer more than the women of other countries. . . . And yet those who are the most secluded and are compelled to lead the most unhealthful lives, are absolutely debarred from any medical relief unless it can be brought them by women. . . . There is one point on which, however, I would like to make the matter clear to you. Personally, I sympathize warmly with medical missions and medical missionaries; but the money subscribed to the national association of which I am the trustee is entirely devoted to *secular* medical work, and it has been subscribed on the understanding that the work of the association should be strictly unsectarian. There is in this great country room and to spare for both missionary and non-missionary organizations."

American women will be interested to know that Lady Curzon, who, by virtue of her office as vicereine of India, has now become president of the Lady Dufferin Fund, enters with energy and sympathy upon this work. While all must welcome the humane labors of the association, it remains to be said that the fact that those who accept its scholarships and work in its hospitals and dispensaries *are not allowed to speak of Christ* in their professional work, remains a serious drawback to its power for good.

ILLUSTRATIVE SELECTIONS

The Song of the Women

(Written for the Lady Dufferin Fund for Medical Aid to the Women of India)

How shall she know the worship we would do her!
  The walls are high, and she is very far.
How shall the women's message reach unto her
  Above the tumult of the packed bazaar?
Free wind of March against the lattice blowing,
Bear thou our thanks, lest she depart unknowing.

Go forth across the fields we may not roam in;
  Go forth beyond the trees that rim the city,
To whatsoe'er fair place she hath her home in,
  Who dowered us with wealth of love and pity;
Out of our shadow pass and seek her, singing,
"I have no gifts but love alone for bringing."

Say that we be a feeble folk who greet her,
  But old in grief, and very wise in tears;
Say that we, being desolate, entreat her
  That she forget us not in after years;
For we have seen the light, and it were grievous
To dim that dawning if our lady leave us.

By life that ebbed with none to stanch the failing,
  By love's sad harvest garnered in the spring,
When love in ignorance wept unavailing
  O'er young buds dead before their blossoming;
By all the gray owl watched, the pale moon viewed,
In past grim years, declare our gratitude!

By hands uplifted to the gods that hear not,
  By gifts that found no favor in their sight,
By faces bent above the babe that stirred not,
  By nameless horrors of the stifling night,
By ills foredone, by peace, her toils discover,
Bid earth be good beneath and heaven above her.

Go forth, O wind, our message on thy wings,
  And they shall hear thee pass and bid thee speed,—
In reed-roofed hut, or white-walled home of kings,—
  Who have been helpen by her in their need.
All spring shall give thee fragrance, and the wheat
Shall be a tasselled floor cloth to thy feet.

Haste, for our hearts are with thee; take no rest,
  Loud-voiced ambassador, from sea to sea.
Proclaim the blessing, manifold, confest,
  Of those in darkness, by her hand set free;
Then very softly to her presence move,
And whisper, "Lady, lo, they know and love!"

—RUDYARD KIPLING.

PRAYER OF A CHILD-WIDOW

O Father of the world, hast Thou not created us? Or has, perchance, some other god made us? Dost Thou care only for men? Hast Thou no thought for us women? Why hast Thou created us male and female? O Almighty, hast Thou not power to make us other than we are, that we, too, might have some share in the comforts of this life? O God, Almighty and Unapproachable, think upon Thy mercy, which is a vast sea, and remember us. O Lord, save us, for we cannot bear our hard lot; many of us have killed ourselves, and we are still killing ourselves. O God of mercy, our prayer to Thee is this, that the curse may be removed from the women of India.

ANN HASSELTINE JUDSON

She who, at Ava and at Oung-pen-la,
  Won brutal men to softness by her grace,
  Illumined prison glooms with her sweet face,
And on despair shone like a morning star,

Her self, her story, and her sufferings won
  Homage from men, as if she came from heaven,
  In whose stout hearts she left a little leaven,
Whose sacred working may outlive the sun.

— W. C. Richards.

Hinduism from Within

I beg of my western sisters not to be satisfied with looking on the outside beauty of the grand philosophies, and not to be charmed with hearing the long and interesting discourses of our educated men, but to open the trap-doors of the great monuments of ancient Hindu intellect, and enter into the dark cellars, where they will see the real workings of the philosophies which they admire so much. Let our western friends come to India and live right among us. Let them frequently go to the hundreds of sacred places where countless pilgrims throng yearly. Let them go round the strongholds of Hinduism and seats of sacred learning, where the Mahatmas and Sadhus dwell, and where the "sublime" philosophies are daily taught and followed. There they will find that the men who boast superior Hindu spirituality oppress widows and trample the poor under their heels. They have deprived the widows of their birthright to enjoy pure life and lawful happiness. They send out hundreds of emissaries to look for young widows, and bring them by thousands to the sacred cities to rob them of their money and their virtue. The so-called sacred places — those veritable hells on earth — have become the graveyards of countless widows and orphans, but not a philosopher or Mahatma has come out boldly to champion their cause. — Pundita Ramabai.

Plea of a Native Hindu Lady

If you English and American ladies accomplish nothing else in India, be sure and do all you can to break up the custom of early marriage.

The Facies of Life

One interesting fact regarding our hospital patients may be taken as absolutely true: the change in face undergone by those who are learning about Christ. I have seen this over and over again, and, on asking others, they have told me the same thing. Their faces seem positively plastic under the moulding of the Holy Spirit. The dull, unintelligent look that so many of the quite ignorant wear on first coming into the wards changes in as short a period as two or three weeks into a far more intelligent and brighter "*facies*," to use a medical term. We doctors speak of the *facies Hippocratici* and the *facies* of this or that disease, but, thank God! this is a *facies* of life, everlasting life, and not of death or disease.

— From the *Church Missionary Intelligencer*, 1901.

Scenes among Missionaries — A Traveller's Views of them and what they are doing

"Travellers in India," remarked my friend, with his cheery smile, "report us missionaries as living in luxury, waited on by troops of servants, demoralizing native simplicity by an impracticable morality, and that the upshot of our work is to make them hypocritically profess a faith they don't believe in in order to curry favor, and to ruin them with the vices of civilization instead of saving them with its virtues. Well, now you have a chance to see how it is for yourself."

The household consisted of the missionary and his wife and a young lady who was assisting them; three or four immaculate Mohammedan servants, at wages of from one to two dollars a month; a horse and buggy; a chapel; and within the walls of the compound some ranges of neat buildings for the accommodation of the native children who were supported and instructed by the mission.

The family sat down thrice a day to a wholesome but Spartan meal. The husband worked with all his might from dawn to dark, and after dark in his study, helping distress, averting evil, enlightening ignorance, and praying with heart and soul to the God and Christ, who was more real to him than any earthly thing. His lovely, artless, human, holy wife, with faith like a little child's, and innocent as a child, yet wise and steadfast in all that touched her work, labored as untiringly and selflessly as her husband. There were perhaps a hundred native children, either orphaned or deserted, who had begun to get flesh on their bones and were busy and happy in learning to read and write their native language, and in singing hymns of praise to the new living God who loves children, and in listening to stories of this same God's loving dealings with His children. They also learned for the first time in their lives what it was to be clean, to be regularly and abundantly fed, and to be treated with intelligent and unselfish affection. These children would have died of the famine had not the mission found and saved them. But though the surroundings and influences were of the loveliest Christian kind, there was no trace of that fanatical hunger for nominal converts — that blind eagerness to fasten the badge of the cross on the sleeve, whether or not it were in the heart — which has often been ascribed to missionary work. From first to last, during my sojourn in India, I saw many native Christians. Those that I saw are a remarkable and impressive body of men and women. I was always saying to myself, "They are like the people of the Bible." Some wore European dress, others did not. Their aspect was gentle, sincere, and modest. Cleanliness is one of the distinguishing marks of the homes of native Christians in India.

One morning we went to an outlying village to visit a native preacher, spending an hour at his house. The women of his family were modestly silent, unless they were questioned directly. They were very gentle and happy-looking women; the expression in their faces was quite different from that of the pagan women. Their eyes met my eyes with a soft, trustful, guileless look. I felt respect and tenderness for them. A little apart squatted an old woman, one of the skeletons. But for the mission support she must have died. She had suffered the extreme of misery; there was nothing left in the world of whatever had been hers; but she seemed to feel the assurance that, living or dead, she would henceforth be taken care of, and not robbed and outraged any more. So long as she lived she could come here twice a day and be fed and gently treated. She did not know what Christianity was, but she knew that its effects on her were good.

Behind the others, in a drooping posture, with her grievous young face bent down, sat a widow with her child. To the people of her own race and creed she was an accursed thing, to be used like a dog. She had survived her husband, and now any man who deigned to touch her uncleanly worthlessness might dispose of her at his pleasure; she had no rights. Her very child, should it live long enough to comprehend her position, would turn from her in contempt. The curse of thousands of years weighed her down, and she believed in its justice as much as did any of them. She could not understand why these Christians treated her with so much kindness.—JULIAN HAWTHORNE.

The threshold weeps for forty days when a girl is born.—*Arabic Proverb.*

THE POINT OF VIEW

It is the fond and patriotic ambition of the son of wealthy parents in Britain to serve his country in India, Africa, or China, either as soldier or civil servant. When the boy goes out to this service, no mother considers it a sacrifice, no father thinks his son has acted like a fool. Yet he goes to face danger, often death. He has to be largely supplied from the parental fortune to sustain the honor of his regiment. He does not go to make money.

Christians of wealth and rank consider it an honor and a privilege to send their sons abroad for such a purpose. To equip and endow a son for this service is no sacrifice, no hardship. But when it is proposed to do the same for missionary service, they reverse every principle of their former action. Foreign service is dangerous to health; it is a great sacrifice to send the young people from home. It is even considered a lowering of the social status; and the rich Christian father who would boast of his son's appointment to a crack regiment or a diplomatic mission would lament his ordination to a medical mission or a foreign college.

Many a rich Christian mother would regard a daughter as hopelessly lost to society by taking up zenana work in India or medical service in China; but she would be delighted to send her to either country as the wife of an officer or civil servant. Climate would be robbed of its terrors if "prospects" were bright for a fashionable career. — DAVID BEATON.

"Where wast Thou sick, Lord, and we knew it not?
Had we but known, how swift had been our feet
To bear us to Thy couch! Ah! service sweet
To watch beside Thee in the dreariest spot."
"Far off I lay, in heathen lands forgot
By thee and all. The blood of lepers beat
In the poor limbs. . . . The sun
Shone in an Indian room; thou didst not see
My form on that bare floor. Those broken hearts
Thou didst not bind. For that thou hast not done
It unto those, thou didst it not to Me." — E. F. F.

When I find a field too hard for a man, I put in a woman. We have grand men; but of forty stations that I have opened in wild heathen nations, eight of them are manned by female heroines. — BISHOP TAYLOR.

Until all Christian women have learned that the cross of Christ is not to be sung about nor wept over, nor smothered in flowers, but set up in the midst of our pleasures; that our Lord never commanded us to cling to that cross, but to carry it, the work of the missionary circle will not be done, nor its warfare accomplished.

— HELEN B. MONTGOMERY.

I have been in India twenty years, and if I had twenty lives to live I would give them all for India. There is no work which God has given to woman which exceeds in beauty and grandeur the work which is to be done by women for the women of India.

— MRS. J. C. ARCHIBALD.

THEMES FOR STUDY OR DISCUSSION

I. Ann H. Judson, Burma's Saint.
II. Early Heroines of Indian Missions.[1]
III. Women of Note in Indian Missions during the Last Quarter Century.[1]
IV. Infanticide and Suttee: Purposes and History of Abolition.
V. Comparative Study in Social, Personal, and Mental Characteristics of the Native Women, Hindu, Mohammedan, Eurasian, and Parsi.
VI. Native Medical, Sanitary, and Hygienic Practices.
VII. "Clinical Christianity."
VIII. The Story of Mary Reed.
IX. Notable Native Christians (Women).
X. Poona; its Christian Schools and India's Child Widows.
XI. The Countess of Dufferin Association.
XII. Native College Women in India and what they are Doing.

BOOKS OF REFERENCE

General reference as for preceding chapter. In addition: Dennis's "Christian Missions and Social Progress," Fuller's "Wrongs of Indian Womanhood," and Storrow's "Our Sisters in India." "Woman's Work for Woman," in Vol. II, "Encyclopædia of Missions," is especially useful on this chapter.

For particular reference on themes given above: —

Barnes's "Between Life and Death," III, V, VI, VII.
Miss Butler's "William Butler."
Carus-Wilson's "Life of Irene Petrie," III, V.

[1] Let each society study the heroines of other denominations as well as its own.

Chamberlain's "The Cobra's Den," VII.
Chapman's "Sketches of Distinguished Indian Women," V, IX, XII.
Dall's "Dr. Anandibai Joshee," VI, VII, IX.
Dyer's "Pundita Ramabai," IX, X.
Mrs. Gracey's "Eminent Missionary Women," I, II, III, VIII.
Mrs. Gracey's "Woman's Medical Work," II, III, VI, VII.
Hopkins' "Within the Purdah," VI, VII.
Humphreys' "Gems of India" (Native Women of Distinction), V.
Hurst's "Indika," X, XI, XII.
Jackson's "Mary Reed, Missionary to the Lepers," VIII.
Judson's "Life of Adoniram Judson," I, II.
Leonowens's "Life and Travel," V.
Lowe's "Medical Missions," VI, VII.
Pierson's "Forward Movements of the Last Half Century," X.
Pitman's "Missionary Heroines," III.
Ramabai's "High-caste Hindu Widow," IV, X.
Miss Sorabji's "Love and Life behind the Purdah," IV, V, XII.
Thoburn's "India and Malaysia," III, V, IX, XI, XII.
"Sooboonagam Ammal," V, IX.
Williamson's "The Healing of the Nations," VI, VII.

INDIA HAS

30 centuries . . . growth for Hinduism.
288,000,000 . . . population.
333,000,000 . . . heathen deities (estimated).
8,400,000 . . . reincarnations for the soul in popular belief.
246,000,000 . . . of the population who can neither read nor write.
144,000,000 . . . women who can neither read nor write.
40,000,000 . . . women secluded in zenanas.
11,573 . . . devadasis in Madras presidency alone in 1881.
6,000,000 . . . wives under 14 years.
2,500,000 . . . wives under 10 years.
27,000,000 . . . widows.
250,000 . . . widows under 14 years.
14,000 . . . widows under 4 years.
25 per cent of Hindu women who die prematurely through effects of early marriage.
25 per cent more who are invalided by the same cause.
500,000 . . . lepers.
50,000,000 . . . outcasts or pariahs.
500,000 . . . persons to every physician, government servants included.
433,000 . . . souls in Haidarabad to each missionary.
20,000,000 . . . souls in Behar unreached by Christian influence.
One century . . growth for Protestant Christianity.
Half a century . enlightened British rule.
21,855 . . . miles of railroad.
18,000 . . . miles of canals for navigation and irrigation.
50,000 . . . miles of macadamized roads.
30,000 . . . miles of telegraph.
150,000 . . . institutions of learning, English and vernacular.

Continued from page 231.

5,000,000	students, of whom 400,000 are female.	
30,000	university students (of whom but 7 per cent are Mohammedan).	
1,380	B.A. degrees conferred in 1897.	
6,000	volumes published yearly.	
1,000,000	women treated in 1897 by Dufferin Fund.	
122	hospitals,	under Christian missionary control.
264	dispensaries,	
184	fully qualified physicians,	
65	asylums for lepers and children of lepers,	
1,800	evangelistic missionaries.	
6,770	native Christian workers, male and female, ordained and unordained.	
2,923,349	Christians of every name.	
41	Protestant missionary publishing houses.	
145	Protestant Christian periodicals.	
84	tongues into which portions of Bible have been translated.	
391	branches of Y. M. C. A. and Y. W. C. A.	
397	societies of Y. P. C. E.	
10 per cent	increase of Hinduism	1881–1891.
10 per cent	increase of Mohammedanism	
20 per cent	increase of Christianity	

CHAPTER VI

FORCES OF DARKNESS AND FORCES OF LIGHT

"He calleth to me out of Seir: 'Watchman, what of the night? Watchman, what of the night?' The watchman said, 'The morning cometh.'"

We have now reached the point from which we must seek to estimate, in view of what has been accomplished in India for good and for God, what obstacles confront us and what grounds we have for both anxiety and good cheer. It is a study in *chiaroscuro*, the clear obscure, for India is a land of twilight, where night and day are struggling in long conflict. It rests with Christian England and Christian America, under God, to determine whether the forces of light shall prevail.

We have seen that England, with its civilizing power, has been politically supreme in India for a century and a half, and for more than a century European and American Christians have been carrying the Christ-light into the gloom.

The conversion of India from idolatry, which must soon follow the noble work of the last century, if western Christendom but awakens to its present opportunity and crisis, is in a peculiar sense the enterprise immediately before the church. India is the key to the eastern world; the point of vantage which, once gained, will command all Asia; the strategic position to win. It has been called the "Gibraltar of Paganism" and the "Rudder of Asia." In it are met the great races, the great languages, the great religions of the Oriental world, and these are held under the central control of a great Anglo-Saxon power. Buddhism, Parseeism, Islam, and Hinduism can all be grappled with on this one field as they can be nowhere else. The English speech and the English civilization form media of communication throughout the vast peninsula. Missions and missionaries are therefore under powerful protection, and are furnished with facilities for the prosecution of their work beyond what can be found in any other Asiatic land. "The complete conquest of the Brahman and Mohammedan of India by the cross," says George Smith, "will be to all Asia what the submission of Constantine was to the Roman empire." If there is faltering, reaction, relaxed effort at this crisis, however, not only is the present opportunity lost, but the fruits of the past and the hopes of the future are lost also.

Light is shining in India, but the great central gloom, into which its rays have not yet penetrated, must sober us, and check too sanguine expectation.

I. CONDITIONS WHICH MAKE FOR THE CONTINUANCE OF DARKNESS IN INDIA

An Alloyed Christianity

We must first name a widely prevailing class of professing Christians at home, men and women of a narrow type of religious life and a shallow type of religious devotion, of whom it may be sadly admitted: —

> "They lived for themselves, they thought for themselves, —
> For themselves and none beside, —
> As if Jesus Christ had never lived,
> And as if he had never died."

Perhaps we may more definitely say: The indifferent, the self-centred American Christian (for we must confine ourselves to those we know best) is the greatest obstacle to the conversion of India, for the unit of foreign missionary enterprise is the unit of personal religion. "Ye are the salt of the earth, but if the salt hath lost its savor, wherewith shall it be salted?"

Foreign Missions not Fashionable

There is undeniably a deep-seated and widespread indifference to the missionary work of the church, abiding strangely side by side with a revival of altruistic energy in certain humanitarian directions in our own country. Social settlement work, for instance, in New York or

Chicago, receives a cordial hearing in circles where the sublimest social settlement work ever attempted by men and women — the lifelong residence of refined and cultured Christian people among the foul and abhorrent scenes of heathendom, in Christ's name — is utterly ignored, and its claims are passed by with cold and slighting indifference. Whether this fact argues more strongly the lack of knowledge, the lack of imagination, or the lack of broad sympathies, might be worth discussing. The condition exists, and is manifested in many forms. Foreign missions have never been a fashionable charity. They are too profoundly in earnest, too irrevocable in the surrender for which they call, too searching in the self-denial.

Wealth and Luxury

All students of our time agree that never in the history of the country was such emphasis laid on the gaining of wealth by men, on the enjoyment of material luxury by women, as now. Everything is rated by its money value. This is the shadow upon American life. Self-denial, willingly practised for the sake of others a generation ago, is fallen out of fashion in the life of to-day, for it wilts like a plucked-up plant under the fierce heat of mammon worship and passion for the power that money can give. "The moral sag" of humanity is sadly observable as we look around us to-day and see the mercenary and selfish aims of young men whose fathers or grandfathers consecrated all they had to the service of Christ and humanity. With wealth and the love of luxury and display, in dress and in social life, has come the craving for amusement and diversion as occupations, not incidents. It is needless to enumerate the varied forms in which this craving for diversion is embodied; the extraordinary vogue through almost all classes of society of card-playing for prizes, sufficiently attests it. Numberless women's clubs in our cities and towns contribute to the manifold complexity of modern social life as well as to *the divided mind* and the shallow thinking which neutralize the missionary spirit. Minds thus prepared to seek an easy escape from serious responsibility for the world's uplifting are ripe for the seed thought which will not fail to fall into such soil, viz., that each ethnic religion is the best adapted to its own people; Hinduism for the Hindus, Islam for the Mohammedans, etc. Why should Occidental peoples seek to force their religion on reluctant nations well satisfied with their own faith? Close following this fatal fallacy of selfishness comes a curiosity, half idle, half morbid, to dip into these other religions a little, while dipping (also a little) into nearly everything else, and in brief time we have our Christian women prattling of the beauties of Buddhism, and the unspeakable elevation of

Hindu philosophy, led on by Madam Blavatsky, Annie Besant, and their followers.

Reaction upon Foreign Missions of Theosophy and Kindred Cults

It would be well for the women who still call themselves Christian, but who like to hover about the seething caldron of heathenism, to be reminded of the stern consequences upon India which their disloyalty to their Lord involves. The earth is not so large as it used to be. Electricity and steam have almost annihilated time and space, and what goes on in secluded drawing-rooms of Boston and New York is known erelong in the homes of Brahmans in Calcutta and Bombay.

"How do you dare to come over here and preach Christianity to us?" is the question now frequently addressed to our missionaries all over India, "when we are told that in your own country many of the people consider our Hindu religion better than their own?"—"Over and over," a missionary newly returned from India told the writer recently, "has this question been put to me, until I have gone home and cried my heart out for sheer discouragement."

Have not our missionaries enough to bear without this treacherous betrayal on the part of their fellow-Christians at home? Let every woman remember that when she patronizes lectures on "the Occult," flatters Swamis, and espouses theosophic subtleties, she is not only weakening by so much the progress of the saving knowledge of our Lord Jesus Christ, but she is by so much strengthening the loathsome, degrading, and licentious rites of the Hindu system, and furthering the reactionary movement away from reform and back to Hinduism, which has arisen among certain circles in India where Mrs. Besant's influence has been felt.

Says the *Indian Social Reformer:* "Mrs. Besant is mainly responsible for much of the mischievous results of the reactionary movement. She upheld the most grotesque practices; she idealized some of the least useful customs of Hindu society. Her sex, her eloquence, her antecedents, her nationality, all told in her favor. . . . *Mrs. Besant has been a retrograde engine to the Hindu race, and the deadening effects of her influence have been felt not only in social reform, but along all lines of national activity.*"

American women, whatever their creed, may well pause before enlisting under that banner! It is common for the imitators of Mrs. Besant to even defend the customs of polygamy and child-marriage, and the cruelties of child-widowhood, and in idle dilettanteism, those who at heart know better accept the defence and gladly drop all further sense of responsibility. "It is hard for us workers in India," says Robert P. Wilder, "to find that the foe is employing against us weapons forged in Christian countries."

The Comparative Meagreness of Money Contributions toward Foreign Missions

As wealth has increased in the United States, a new type of pleasure and luxury-loving women have been evolved, as we have seen, following many fads and spending money for social and domestic gratification with unparalleled profusion. Along with this, a marked tendency to exalt intellectual attainment and a species of worship of higher education have arisen. These tendencies have led to the most magnificent endowment and enrichment by Christian capitalists of all means and institutions for intellectual progress at home, but without accompanying or commensurate increase of gifts for the Christianizing or uplifting of the heathen world. One of the wealthiest and most influential denominations in the country reports 2224 of its churches as giving absolutely nothing last year to Foreign Missions. Another great denomination reports 5400 churches out of 10,000.

It is evident that India cannot be won for Christ without constant advance into new fields and constant additions to the working force. In place of this, in place of seizing strategic points at which to plant new centres of light and influence, in place of seeing the royal banners forward go, the dull, heart-breaking watchword ever passed from sentinel to sentinel all along the line of darkened India is:

"Retrench! retrench! No money in the treasury! Call back the flag!"

The Son of God goes forth to war, but his church at large deserts at the pinch those who follow in his train, and watches them a moment with cold indifference as they climb the steep ascent alone, with peril, toil, and pain, and then turns back unmoved to the farm, to the merchandise, to the counting-room, and the card-table.

Should the Christian business men of America once take upon their hearts the indescribable suffering and degradation of India's millions, never again need that ignominious, that shameful word "Retrench" (Retreat) be passed around the fainting land.

We have considered several leading causes resident in our own land which contribute their force to keep the light of Christ out of India. We will turn next to India itself and glance at certain hindrances peculiar to the conditions existing there, outside of the broad, general facts of heathenism itself. Among these difficulties we will briefly mention: —

Interested Motives and Incomplete Conversion of Natives

There is a tendency among the lower classes, in their extreme poverty and superstition, to welcome missions, and perhaps especially medical missions, for the material advantage gained, simply adding to their many divinities another who for the time seems to respond more signally than the earlier ones to their petitions for temporal relief.

Self-sufficiency of Brahmanism

Next, a confidence in the superiority of their own religion to all others, always met with among Brahmans, professing as they do to have gone far beyond the Christian's conception. One of them declared in this country: "If a minute history of India could be written for the last six thousand years, there would be descriptions of many miracles performed by our sages as remarkable as any attributed to Christ. The Hindu can himself confidently hope some day, on this very earth, clothed in flesh and blood, to become Christ."

Furthermore, the great and growing student body in the five universities (the largest in the Orient) is very largely made up of Brahmans. There are, for instance, four times as many Brahman as non-Brahman graduates from Madras University, although the Brahman population is not one-fifth of the whole population. The Brahmans thus possess the aristocracy both of birth and of learning, and are the recognized leaders. Their intellectual strength and subtlety, combined with the self-confidence already mentioned, which the non-Christian training of the universities in no way weakens but rather increases, make them formidable opponents of Christianity.

Men like these are difficult of access, and can be convinced only by thoroughly trained minds. The loss of position, property, and friends often entailed upon the higher castes if they submit to baptism, is sufficient also to turn aside many. It is not strange that the great ingatherings of the past century have been from among low-caste or non-caste peoples, as the Kols, Karens, and Telugus. While this fact may in the end conduce to the levelling of caste distinctions by the uplifting of Sudras and Pariahs, it remains to be said that to reach the Brahmans adequately and intelligently is at once extremely difficult and extremely necessary.

Caste and Fatalism

Again, the obstinacy of caste and other paralyzing social customs, and the ever present fatalism, create a profound, and in some cases an almost unconquerable, apathy toward new light or life or hope. "Whatever is written upon our own foreheads will come to pass," is a common saying among Hindus as well as Mohammedans; as also, "We must walk according to custom," and "Different religions are roads leading to the same city." The conviction that millions of rebirths await every soul, and the absence of a sense of sinfulness, weaken the force of the Christian motive and appeal.

Good and Evil Influences in the British Occupation

When we now find it necessary to take a cursory view of the British in India, we find a most complex study in the clear-obscure, for here, indeed, light and darkness commingle in bewildering forms. With some things to deplore, there is yet so much in which to rejoice that we may well let this subject occupy the middle ground through which we shall presently pass into the region of light.

It is the fixed and perhaps necessary policy of the government, as we have seen in previous chapters, punctiliously to abstain from any manifestation of sympathy with or explicit furtherance of Christianity in India, or to interfere in any degree with the debasing idolatry of the people. This must always be kept distinctly in mind. British officials are strictly enjoined to "equal and impartial protection" of all forms of worship however immoral; and unless supplemented by missionary endeavor, the English occupation can never affect the heart and conscience of India. The Hindus, to whom religion is a rule of life governing every smallest detail, cannot understand a nation which appears to ignore its own religion. They infer that the British have either no religion or none which is worth putting forward, and a contempt for Christianity thus arises.

New India

As a consequence, then, of the progress of civilization *without Christianity*, we are beginning to see rising out of the dim chaos of old India a new and still pagan India, self-conscious, *knowing*, cynical as regards Christianity, inflated with a sublime sense of its own importance and an overweening opinion of its own sufficiency. This new India is filled with men devoid of moral foundation, who have learned, outwardly at least, to scorn the puerile superstitions of their past, and to blush at the hideous idolatries of the less enlightened of their countrymen, but who have taken into their minds no purer faith, no guiding light of divine love. This condition of things calls urgently for prompt action on the part of the Christian church, upon which is thus laid, in a peculiar sense, the definite responsibility of supplementing Anglo-Saxon civilization with Anglo-Saxon Christianity.

Says the *Indian Witness:* "India cannot wait, simply because in her case waiting means the adoption of European civilization without European Christianity; and the work of moral and spiritual regeneration will be inconceivably more difficult than it would be were the gospel given to her during the days of her transition. . . . If the change is completed without the Bible, and the new civilization of India crystallizes into a godless, irreligious life, it will be almost impossible to make any moral impression upon it by teaching Christian doctrine. It is 'now or never,' almost."

The Opium Trade

The support of the opium trade by the British government in India, the large revenue which it draws from the liquor traffic, its practice of issuing licenses to prostitutes, and the immorality of the army, have been again and again cast in the teeth of Christian missionaries.

The awful results of the opium traffic in India are beginning to arouse the attention of the world. Between five and six thousand tons of opium are sent from India to China annually as an article of English trade, from which the government derives a large annual revenue, while *the former viceroy of India was the largest manufacturer of opium in the world.* China has begged and struggled to be delivered from this curse; and Burma, in which the introduction of opium was prohibited by law until its annexation by the British, was said to be "literally on its knees praying the British government not to introduce the scourge." Christians in England protest and petition, and a harmless resolution condemning the traffic has even been passed in Parliament. Meanwhile the traffic and the habit grow apace. The rate of increase in the consumption of opium in the Bombay presidency alone, according to official reports, has been at the rate of 549 per cent since 1876. The terms of the license to sell the drug fix the *minimum* quantity which *must* be sold under penalty of fine.

"The injury to missions by opium," writes Dennis, "is something incalculable, and the issue between righteousness and humanity on the one hand, and iniquity and callous greed on the other, is both sharp and irrepressible. This traffic in opium has been called 'England's greatest contribution to the world's wretchedness.'"

The conscience of Christian England is restless over the course of the government in this matter, for provision for continuing the recent policy has been incorporated in the new treaty with China, and the supply of opium from India has been guaranteed anew. At a meeting just held in London to oppose the traffic, Sir Joseph Pease, M.P., pointed out that those who deem the opium trade immoral and antagonistic to the principles of true Christianity have to fight the Indian government. The trade, he said, was maintained on the most false of all moral arguments, viz., that if they did not do it, some one else would. Moral retribution, he declared, was as certain as the sunrise.

The old leaven of selfish commercialism belonging to the East India Company has never been wholly eliminated from British rule. This mercenary policy and the moral timidity which it engenders militate seriously against the enlightenment of India.

Mutual Antagonisms of English and Indians

Akin to this, a part indeed of the same thing, is the common, although happily not universal, indifference of the English residents in India to the uplifting of the natives, and the object lessons of worldliness and lax morality set constantly before the eyes of the people in the social life and in the pursuit of pleasure of the "white foreigners." The abstemious Hindu scarcely conceals his contempt for the gross indulgence of his English conquerors in brandy and beer-drinking and in gluttony; for their half-savage love for the chase and the destruction of animal life; for their idolatry of money-getting, eclipsing all nobler pursuits.

On the other hand, the English, whether soldier or civilian, is outspoken in his disgust for the idolatrous, fawning, treacherous natives. "To affect deep interest in things native is *incorrect*," says Isabel Savory, the Indian traveller. "A lady was asked what she had seen of the people since she came out, 'Oh, nothing!' said she. 'Thank goodness, I know nothing at all about them, and don't wish to; really, I think the less one sees and knows about them the better.'" To this common attitude we are glad to believe there are honorable and not infrequent exceptions.

These are some of the darker aspects of British occupation; meanwhile there is much to consider in abatement of these evils. Peace, a wise and firm execution of justice, a highly centralized administration of public affairs, a much lower rate of taxation than under the Mughals, government schools, universities, hospitals, railroads, telegraph systems, a free press, material progress everywhere, mark the Anglo-Saxon rule in India since the middle of the nineteenth century. Moreover, since the proclamation of 1858, the British government has held consistently to its impartial policy, and has protected Christians as well as heathen in the exercise of their religion; it has even of late years invited missionaries to open schools, and has largely withdrawn its patronage of idolatry, although quantities of Hindu idols are still manufactured in England for export. We have already seen that the British government, at the instance of missionaries, has abolished certain of the more horrible of Hindu social and religious crimes, such as suttee, thuggee, female infanticide, human sacrifice, etc. With great energy, indeed, has it aimed to discharge the task of introducing western civil and criminal law, western science, and western industry into its great dependency.

In a sense, all that ministers to the advance of civilization and education furthers the missionary enterprise, at least to the extent of facilitating its external progress and neutralizing the power of superstition. It must, however, be admitted that the railroads which help the missionary to reach a circuit of villages with the good news of the kingdom, also make a hundred-fold easier, and consequently more popular, the attendance on the awful debauchery of Hindu festivals and pilgrimages. That the spread of bare knowledge, unilluminated by spiritual teaching, is powerless to overcome the deep-seated immorality of the race, has been only too abundantly proved; and human souls are not carried into Christ's kingdom by rail and telegraph.

Brahmoism, or Reformed Hinduism

Belonging also in the debatable realm where light and darkness meet, are the various attempts which have been made, since 1830, by native Hindus, to effect a reform of their own religion. Profoundly stirred by the influences of Christianity, filled with new and nobler aspirations for purer worship, and yet not wholly ready to break with their inherited faith, these undoubtedly sincere men have sought to coördinate Hinduism with Christianity and to form an eclectic religion — a composite of the doctrines of the Christian Scriptures, the Veda, Koran, and Zend-Avesta.

Rammohun Roy, the first and most famous of these reformers, established the Brahmo

Somaj, which may be translated the "Church of God," in 1830, at Calcutta. A rationalistic and pantheistic tendency belonged to the movement from the first, to which was added, in 1858, under the guidance of the new champion, Keshub Chunder Sen, the strong effort at social reform, traces of which we have met in a previous chapter. The movement divided quickly into different Somajes, with different shades of belief and points of contention. The leading tenets of the Prarthana Somaj will illustrate both the nobleness and the inadequacy of the whole reform :

1. I believe in one God. 2. I renounce idol worship. 3. I will do my best to lead a moral life. 4. If I commit any sin through the weakness of my moral nature, I will repent of it, and ask the pardon of God.

The omission of Christ from this declaration is characteristic. None of these reformers have given full and hearty allegiance to him as a personal Saviour, and herein lies the pitiful deadness and inadequacy of the effort which has taken but little hold on the Hindu people at large. "The only twice-born men who can change the morals of India for the better are those who are born again by God's Spirit into likeness to Christ." Even Mr. Sen, whose early reform measures enlisted widespread sympathy and admiration, fell, before his death, into most fantastic and deplorable errors.

II. FORCES WHICH ARE BRINGING LIGHT TO INDIA

Revival of the Spirit of Missionary Devotion

Among these forces, which are clear and indubitable in our own country, we recognize, out of the materialism, the mammon and luxury worship, and the selfishness, a new and powerful Renaissance. It is the revival of a perception of the unity of the race, and the brotherhood of men, and a rediscovery of the Law of Service, the Law of Sacrifice, and the Law of Love. To it we owe the invasion of India by the Christian associations both of young men and young women. To it we owe the Student Volunteer Movement, with its well-tempered enthusiasm, its sturdy discipline, and the sublime audacity of its thrilling watchword: "The evangelization of the world in this generation." To this new inspiration we owe it that, from our most prospered families, from colleges and universities, select souls, young men and women of high heart, pure mind, and noble endowment are going forth in great numbers to live their lives amid the darkness of the heathen world. In some cases whole families are doing this in touching and noble unison. Never, perhaps, did the old motto, *Noblesse oblige*, reach to the height of heroism, to the depths of martyrdom, that it measures to-day.

Character of Missionaries

With advancing standards of education at home, the missionaries of to-day are a more thoroughly equipped and disciplined company than in any preceding period; with the opening up of the East, they are coming into the eye of the whole world as never before, and their intellectual achievements, the beauty of their Christlike lives, and the nature of the results of their labor, at last begin in some degree to be apprehended. The unique position of wholly disinterested citizens of India which they occupy, in contrast with other foreigners who are there for trade or other selfish purposes, commands the respect of the whole world. Further than that, this unique position involves offices of trust and of mediation which may be tested and put to the touch in the coming century in ways of which we do not dream to-day. It is probable that in no realm of the heathen world have missionaries the far-reaching power and influence which they have in India, owing to the friendly relations between them and the government. It can fairly be said that every reform of the crimes of Hinduism has been undertaken at the instance of missionaries, from the days of Carey to the present time. One of the greatest of India's statesmen, Lord Lawrence, has said, "In my judgment Christian missions have done more real, lasting good to the peoples of India than all other agencies combined." Everywhere they have led the way, and the government has followed. An American Methodist woman, from a little western New York village, began medical work in 1869 among the women of India, and the Lady Dufferin Fund, under royal patronage, followed. Hannah Marshman, Ann Judson, wives of Baptist missionaries, and the wives of the Bombay American Board pioneers began schools for Indian girls early in the century, and now the Indian government has taken up the work initiated by them.

"Not long ago the burning of a widow on the funeral pyre of her husband was the custom," says Maurice Phillips of the London Society. "Missionaries agitated, and that custom was abolished. Not long ago infanticide was the custom. Missionaries agitated, and that was abolished. Not many years ago civil service and military officers of government attended heathen festivals, not in order to protect them, but in order to add dignity to them. Missionaries agitated, and put an end to that. Not long ago the government managed all the temples, it collected the revenues, it paid the priests, it paid the dancing-girls, the prostitutes of India. Missionaries agitated, and that was abolished. Not long ago converts to Christianity lost their civil rights. Missionaries agitated, and a law was passed that a change of faith did not involve the loss of any civil liberty. Not long ago the government prohibited the women who had embraced Christianity from wearing clothes above their waist.[1] Missionaries agitated, and an order was given that the Christian women should be allowed to dress decently. In this way missionaries watched the proceedings of the government in India. We criticise, we agitate, we petition, and when missionaries petition in a body, they are generally listened to favorably."

Character of Native Converts

Nowhere do we find brighter hope of light for India than in the character of her native Christians from the days of the Mutiny down. Doubts are often cast upon the capacity of the Hindu to accept and assimilate Christianity. Let him who doubts go to India and see quarrelsome, obscene, half-barbarous men transformed into a manhood of dignity, honor, and of self-denying, humble devotion to the good of others; women lifted from sullen, hopeless ignorance and low servility to the sweet and hallowed life of honored and enlightened womanhood. Let him compare the vacant-minded voluptuary of the

[1] The women of the humbler orders in Travancore were formerly forbidden to wear any clothing above the waist; but those who became Christians felt this unbecoming, and began to wear a loose jacket. The caste women regarded this as a gross insult to them, and for years a bitter persecution was carried on, beginning in 1827. It was not until 1859 that the Shanar women were legally permitted to wear an upper cloth.

zenana with the Hindu college girl of to-day. Let him visit the homes of the Christian natives and see the new order, the new grace, the new self-respect which transform them into the norm and type of all that is best in human society. Let him visit the native churches and find them often not only well sustained and *self-supporting*, but already *missionary* churches, giving out of their poverty, with nobly pathetic sacrifice, for the Christianizing of their fellows in heathenism.

The Decay of Hinduism

The lower forms of Hinduism, animistic and demonistic beliefs, are rapidly giving way, while the dry rot at work at the heart of the system is symbolized by the general decay of Hindu temples throughout the country. For this decay Lord Curzon recently called the people to task, a straw which shows how much direct aid Christianity may expect of the British government. New temples when built are on an inferior scale and usually among rural populations. Among the classes influenced by western ideas Hinduism is rapidly breaking up. Said a Hindu: "Hinduism is sick unto death. I am fully persuaded that it must fall." "The younger men do not much mind caste rules, not more than we can help," said another. Hinduism, "by absorption and expansion, has grown into the most gigantic, debasing parody of true religion in existence." Hollow through and through, the day of its downfall must come and cannot tarry.

The Christian Religion

However we may gather courage from the disintegration of heathenism, or from other sources at home and abroad, the supreme hope and the supreme inspiration for India are in the light of the knowledge of the glory of God in the face of Jesus Christ. The story of missions in India is only the process of love at work. For the worker in the half-indifferent church at home, for the missionary on the field, for the native of India just coming into light, there is alike the touch of that—

> "Perfect life in perfect labor writ,
> Of all men's Comrade, Servant, King, and Priest,
> — the crystal Christ."

The law of highest service, that of self-sacrifice, was first made known, to a world which sought its own, on the Cross of Calvary. Slowly has that majestic, sweet, and awful law had its outworking through nineteen centuries. Oriental religions have never conceived of it. They have sacrifice, indeed, but it is the barren sacrifice of selfish asceticism undergone to acquire merit; the pitiful sacrifice of dumb brutes slain to propitiate reluctant gods. It is the surpassing glory and beauty of Christianity that its prime motive is the willing sacrifice of the individual, hoping nothing for himself, in order to bring healing and rescue to his fellow-men. The Cross of Christ is the light of India, the light of the world.

In hoc signo vinces.

ILLUSTRATIVE SELECTIONS

The Church at the Open Door

The revelation of the Orient is the opportunity of the missionary. Hitherto he has been fitfully revealed by the accident of important events or had in memory by religious conventicles alone. He, too, comes into the range of secular vision. His seclusion is at an end. What he is, what he does, and what he knows will be matter of solicitude as he turns the eyes of the conscience of Christianity upon the practices and transactions about him. He may not desire it, but he is the accredited censor of foreign residents and policies. He is the witness of the West in the heart of the East. He cannot hide himself if he would. He stands in the full blaze of publicity for criticism or approval. His office of mediation between the East and West is immensely enlarged. He is at a railway terminus and in reach of the telegraph. His stores of information will be demanded in every political difficulty and in every emergency and abuse of trade, and he cannot withhold his knowledge. He must testify at the council board of the powers, and his information will be indispensable to statesmen. He is henceforth a part of the world's bureau of intelligence. — B. D. Hahn.

Dawn

The opened world — the simplified faith! Surely this of all times is not the time to disbelieve in foreign missions; surely he who despairs of the power of the gospel to convert the world to-day, despairs of the noontide just when the sunrise is breaking out of twilight on the earth. Distance has ceased to be a hindrance. Language no longer makes men total strangers. A universal commerce is creating common bases and forms of thought. For the first time in the history of the world there is a manifest, almost an immediate possibility of a universal religion. No wonder that at such a time the missionary spirit, which had slumbered for centuries, should have sprung upon its feet, and the last fifty years should have been one of the very greatest epochs in missionary labor in the whole history of the world. — BISHOP PHILLIPS BROOKS.

THE TESTIMONY OF AN EXPERT

Beyond doubt the missionaries have a great repute for goodness, for charity, for devotion to duty throughout the heathen world; they have *done much to raise our national character;* to remove doubts regarding our wars, our politics, and our administration, and to soften the memories of many unhappy events, which, from various causes, have come to pass during the nineteenth century. I know that you will occasionally hear opinions contrary to those which I am now most positively pronouncing. You will hear the mission cause decried, and the results of the mission disparaged, whereas I say that these results are *fully commensurate with all the efforts you have made*, that the reports you receive are worthy of entire acceptance, their only defect being that they cannot give you the impression of the beauty and excellence of the work as it is indelibly fixed in my own mind. Indeed, I am myself at this moment hopeless of conveying to you the glowing images which I have in my own thoughts of Protestant missions of all denominations, and I have been acquainted more or less with all the missions from Cape Comorin to the Himalayas, — the fairest and finest field now in the non-Christian world for Christian evangelization. — The Right Hon. SIR RICHARD TEMPLE, *formerly Lieutenant-Governor of Bengal, Governor of Bombay, and Chief Commissioner of the Central Provinces, November,* 1900.

The War Spirit

Whatever harms love harms missions. Hence it is perfectly plain that the warlike spirit, if it takes possession of a people and animates their thought and feeling, is distinctly fatal to the missionary motive. The breaking of the race into warring groups, or groups pledged to the spirit and aim of war, is ruinous to the missionary work. The war feeling toward men and the missionary feeling toward men are opposite and incompatible just so far as they are active and strong. And so we are compelled to say that the recent awakening of the warlike spirit must be counted among the influences that perpetuate the present crisis in missions, and threaten to perpetuate it far into the coming century. — William N. Clarke.

England paid for the war in Afghanistan sixty millions, while one-eighth of that sum was all the entire church of Christ could devote in that same year to the world-wide campaign for Christ. — A. T. Pierson.

Men of Good Will

Widely distributed throughout Christendom, though necessarily hidden from view, are to be found what might be specially named good men — souls who love goodness for its own sake, and are bent toward doing good, as mankind in general is bent toward doing evil. How these souls, charily keeping themselves from the view of the public, are striving to make this world a little better by their efforts and prayers; how they often shed tears for the wretchedness of the state of the people of whom they read only in newspapers; how they lay upon their hearts the welfare of the whole of mankind; and how willing they are to take part in the work of ameliorating human misery and ignorance, — these I saw and witnessed with my own eyes, and can testify to the genuine spirit that underlies them all. These silent men are they who, in their country's peril, are the first to lay down their lives in its service; who, when told of a new mission enterprise in a heathen land, will deliver their railroad fares to the missionaries who undertake it, and return home tramping on their feet, and praise God for their having done so; who, in their big tearful hearts, understand all the mysteries of Divine Mercy, and hence are merciful toward all around them. No fierceness and blind zeal with these men, but gentleness and cool calculation in doing good. Indeed, I can say with all truthfulness that I saw *good* men only in Christendom. Brave men, honest men, righteous men, are not wanting in heathendom; but I doubt whether *good* men, — by that I mean those men summed up in that one English word which has no equivalent in other language, "Gentleman," — I doubt whether such are possible without the religion of Jesus Christ to mould us. "The Christian, God Almighty's gentleman" — he is a unique figure in this world, indescribably beautiful, noble, and lovable. — KANZO UCHIMURA.

A HINDU OPINION OF MRS. BESANT

When an English lady (as, for instance, Mrs. Besant) of decent culture professes to be an admirer of Tantric mysticisms and Krishna worship, it behooves every well-wisher of the country to tell her plainly that sensible men do not want her eloquence for gilding what is rotten. In fact, abomination worship is the chief ingredient of modern Hinduism.

— From *Reis and Ruyyet*, Calcutta Hindu newspaper.

Many persons mistake the way in which the conversion of India will be brought about. I believe it will take place wholesale, just as our own ancestors were converted. — SIR CHARLES TREVELYAN.

Appeal to Christians in America

The churches now, as in all former ages, deem it right and highly commendable for some of Christ's disciples to renounce all prospects of worldly emolument and ease, to commit themselves and their families, if they have any, under Providence into the hands of charity; — to forego the comforts and endearments of civilized society and Christian friends; to brave every danger, whether from the raging billows of the ocean, the sickly climate, or the sanguinary barbarian, and to meet death in whatever time, place, or form it may be allotted them — and all this for the sake of preaching Christ to the heathen. By *approving* and, as is the fact, *requiring* this of their missionaries, they do virtually bind themselves to make corresponding sacrifices and exertions to the same end. I am not pleading that missionaries should be eased of their burdens or alleviated in their sacrifices. No, I plead with Christians that they would act consistently. I entreat them to behold in what they *require* of their missionaries the measure of their own duty to Christ and to the heathen. Until a principle of action more commensurate with other duty enjoined is adopted, and the work of evangelizing the heathen is more equally shared among Christians generally, as was the fact in the first ages of the church, we have no good reason to expect that the world will be converted.

— Gordon Hall, Bombay, 1826.

The greatest hindrances to the evangelization of the world are those within the church. — John R. Mott.

Christ's Ambassador

The missionary appears to me to be the highest type of human excellence in the nineteenth century, and his profession to be the noblest. He has the enterprise of the merchant, without the narrow desire of gain; the dauntlessness of the soldier, without the shedding of blood; the zeal of the geographical explorer, but for a higher motive than science. And if there is anything greater than an English missionary, it is an American.

— ROBERT N. CUST, ESQ.

Cablegram from English and American Student Volunteers: —

India never before so open, so ripe, so hopeful, so critical, so needy as now. India prays for the awakening of America to look, pray, send, and come for her awakening.

Lahore, Punjab, February, 1898.

O Thou, that from eternity
Upon Thy wounded heart hast borne
Each pang and cry of misery
Wherewith our human hearts are torn,

Thy love upon the grievous cross
Doth glow, the beacon-light of time,
Forever sharing pain and loss
With every man in every clime.

How vast, how vast Thy sacrifice,
As ages come and ages go,
Still waiting, till it shall suffice,
To draw the last cold heart and slow.

— HENRY N. DODGE.

None but Jesus, none but Jesus deserves to wear the bright and glorious diadem of India, and Jesus Christ shall have it. — KESHUB CHUNDER SEN.

PRAYER FOR INDIA, BURMA, AND CEYLON

O God, who hast made of one blood all nations of men to dwell upon the face of Thy whole earth, and who didst send Thy blessed Son to preach peace to them that are afar off and to them that are nigh, grant that all the people of Hindu, Buddhist, and Mohammedan lands may feel after Thee and find Thee; and hasten, O Lord, the fulfilment of Thy promise to pour out Thy Spirit upon all flesh.

O Lord God, who rulest in the kingdoms of men and givest them to whomsoever Thou wilt, we present our humble supplications before Thee in behalf of India. Make us faithful, we beseech Thee, in so great a trust. Give us a spirit of true compassion for the multitudes in that land who yet walk in darkness and the shadow of death. Suffer them no longer to bow down to idols which their own hands have made. Lead them from the corrupt worship of false gods to worship Thee in the beauty of holiness. Have pity on their blindness, their misplaced confidence, their mistaken zeal, their self-inflicted sufferings. Teach them the pure mystery of the Incarnation of Thy blessed Son. Deliver them from their dread of the powers of darkness. Raise up among them, O Lord, teachers of Thy truth, who may lead them to embrace the holy faith of Thy Church; for Thy mercy's sake, through Jesus Christ our Lord. AMEN.

THEMES FOR STUDY OR DISCUSSION

I. India as a Point of Vantage in winning the Eastern World to Christ.
II. Missions in India as Social Settlements.
III. Material, Intellectual, and Political Improvement in India under British Rule.
IV. Dangers of Civilization without Christianity.
V. Question for Debate: Should the British Viceroy urge the Hindus to keep their Temples in Repair?
VI. What should be the Attitude of Christian Women toward Theosophy and Kindred Cults?
VII. Native Hindu Reformers.
VIII. Where does the Responsibility for the Enlightenment of India's Millions rest?
IX. Contrast between the Timidity of many Indian Politicians and the Courage of Indian Missionaries.
X. What may be involved to a High-caste Hindu in making a Public Christian Confession?
XI. The Missionary Enterprise and the Kingdom of God.
XII. The Religion of Christ the Supreme Revelation.

BOOKS OF REFERENCE

General Reference as for Preceding Chapter

Bell's "British Rule in India," III.
Bushnell's "Nature and the Supernatural," XII.
Clarke's "Study of Christian Missions," VIII, X, XII.
Dennis's "Foreign Missions after a Century," IV, VIII, IX, X, XII.
Ellinwood's "Oriental Religions and Christianity," VII, XII.
Fuller's "Wrongs of Indian Womanhood," VI, VII, IX.

Gates's "Christian Missions and the Use of Wealth," VIII, XI.

Gordon's "The Holy Spirit in Missions," VIII, XI, XII.

Martin's "Apostolic and Modern Missions," XI, XII.

Mason's "Little Green God," VI.

Mott's "Evangelization of the World in this Generation," VIII, XI, XII.

Mott's "Strategic Points in the World's Conquest," I, IV, VIII.

Pierson's "Crisis of Missions," I, VIII, IX, XI, XII.

Pierson's "Divine Enterprise of Missions," VIII, XI, XII.

Ram Chundra Bose's "Brahmoism," VI, VII.

Robbins's "Handbook of India," III.

Smith's "Conversion of India," I, III, VII, VIII, XI.

Speer's "Missions and Politics in Asia," III, IV, VIII, IX.

Strong's "New Era," VIII.

Strohg's "Next Great Awakening," XI.

Temple's "India in 1880," III, V, VIII.

Warneck's "Modern Missions and Culture," IV, IX.

Wilder's "Among India's Students," I, III, IV, VII, X.

Sir M. Williams's "Modern India and the Indians," III, V.

Sir M. Williams's "Religious Thought and Life in India," V, VII.

APPENDIX

LIST OF TWENTY BOOKS

At Moderate Prices, Most Useful in Course of Study on India

"Between Life and Death." I. H. Barnes. Marshall Bros., London. 3s. 6d.

"Brief History of the Indian Peoples." Sir W. W. Hunter. H. Frowde, 91 Fifth Avenue. 256 pp. $0.90.

"Christian Missions and Social Progress." J. S. Dennis. Fleming H. Revell Co. 3 vols. Each vol. $2.50.

"Conversion of India." George Smith. Fleming H. Revell Co. $1.50.

"Ecumenical Miss. Conference Report, 1900." American Tract Society. 2 vols. $1.50.

"Encyclopædia of Missions." E. M. Bliss. Funk and Wagnalls. 2 vols. $12.00.[1]

"Handbook of Comparative Religion." S. H. Kellogg. Westminster Press. Paper, 30 cents; cloth, 75 cents.

"High Caste Hindu Woman." Pundita Ramabai. Fleming H. Revell Co. $0.75.

"Hinduism." Sir Monier Williams. Young & Co., Cooper Institute. $1.00. (An abridgment of "Religious Thought and Life.")

"Hindu Literature." E. A. Reed. Scott, Forseman Co., Chicago. $1.50.

[1] While the price of these volumes is relatively high, they will prove a good investment as being equally indispensable for the study of all missionary subjects.

"India and Malaysia." J. M. Thoburn. Hunt and Eaton. $1.50.

"In India." G. W. Steevens. Dodd, Mead and Co. $1.50.

"Life of Adoniram Judson." Edward Judson. American Baptist Publication Society. $1.25.

"Men of Might in India Missions." H. E. Holcomb. Fleming H. Revell Co. $1.25.

"Missionary Expansion since the Reformation." J. A. Graham. Fleming H. Revell Co. $1.25. (With eight colored maps and 145 illustrations.)

"Mosaics from India." M. B. Denning. Fleming H. Revell Co. $1.25.

"Our Sisters in India." E. Storrow. Fleming H. Revell Co. $1.25.

"Religious Thought and Life in India." Sir Monier Williams. (Also called "Brahmanism and Hinduism.") Macmillan Co. $3.50

"Short History of India." J. Talboys Wheeler. Macmillan Co. $3.50.

"Wrongs of Indian Womanhood." M. B. Fuller. Fleming H. Revell Co. $1.25.

TWENTY LEADING MISSIONARY PERIODICALS

Assembly Herald (Pres.), U. S.
Baptist Missionary Magazine (A. B. M. U.), U. S.
Chronicle London Missionary Society, England.
Church Missionary Intelligencer (C. M. S.), England.
Foreign Missionary Tidings (Pres.), Canada.
Friends' Missionary Advocate (Friends), U. S.
Helping Hand (W. B. F. M. S.), U. S.
Life and Light for Women (Woman's Board, Cong.), U. S.
Messenger and Record (Pres.), England.
Mission Studies (Board of Interior, Cong.), U. S.
Missionary Gleaner (Dutch Reformed), U. S.
Missionary Herald (Baptist), England.

Missionary Link (Woman's Union), U. S.
Missionary Outlook (M. E.), Canada.
Missionary Review of the World (Interdenominational), U. S.
Missionary Tidings (Christian), U. S.
Spirit of Missions (P. E. Church), U. S.
Woman's Missionary Friend (M. E.), U. S.
Woman's Work for Woman (Pres.), U. S.
Women's Missionary Magazine (United Free Church), Scotland.

WORDS OFTEN MET WITH IN BOOKS ON INDIA

Amin . . . . Head of district.
Anna . . . . Copper coin = $\frac{1}{16}$ of a rupee.
Ayah . . . . Nurse.
Babu . . . . English-speaking native gentleman.
Bakshish . . Fee, gratuity.
Bazar . . . . Street in which are shops.
Bajjan . . . Hymn.
Begum . . . A Mohammedan princess.
Bhisti . . . . Water carrier.
Bibi . . . . . Wife.
Bulbul . . . Indian nightingale.
Bungalow . European residence.
Bunghias . . Sweepers; the lowest caste.
Bunnia . . . Shopkeeper.
Chamars . . Leather workers.
Chaprassi . Attendant, messenger.
Charpoy . . Portable bedstead.
Chela . . . . Disciple.
Chilam . . . Pipe.
Chit . . . . . Written testimonial or message.
Chopatti . . Unleavened bread, universally used.
Chuddar . . Muslin covering for the head.
Compound . Land surrounding bungalow.
Crore . . . . Ten millions.
Dak . . . . . The post, the relay of men.
Dandy . . . Conveyance carried by coolies.
Deodar . . . A kind of cedar.
Dervish . . . Mohammedan fanatic.
Deva . . . . God.
Dhoti . . . . Washerman.

Diwan or Divan .	A council.
Durbar . . .	Court reception.
Gharri . . .	A carriage.
Ghat	A quay or flight of steps leading to the water. Also a steep mountain side.
Ghee	Clarified butter.
Gosain . . .	Member of a Bengali sect.
Guru	Religious teacher.
Hadji	A Mohammedan gentleman who has made the pilgrimage to Mecca.
Hakim . . .	Physician.
Howdah . .	Seat used for riding elephants.
Karma . . .	The law of consequences. Buddhistic.
Khitmutgar	A servant or butler, usually Mohammedan.
Kismet . . .	Destiny.
Kowree . . .	A small white shell used for money among the poorest people.
Lakh	100,000.
Lama	A celibate priest (Buddhist).
Lascar . . .	Servant in charge of tents.
Lat	Monolithic column.
Lota	Metal cooking utensil.
Madrissah .	School.
Maha-	Used in composition, meaning great.
Mahadeva .	Great God, used of Siva.
Mahajan . .	Money lender.
Mahatma . .	An adept of the first order.
Maidan . . .	Plain.
Mela	A fair.
Memsahib .	Lady.
M'lecha . . .	Foreigner, alien.
Moulvie . .	Native Mohammedan teacher.
Munshi . . .	Teacher.
Musjid . . .	Mosque.
Nawab . . .	Mohammedan chief.
Nirvana . .	Oblivion.
Paddy	Rice in the husk.
Padre Sahib	Clergyman or missionary.
Pan	The leaf which encloses the betelnut.
Pani	Water.
Pan supari .	The betelnut.
Patel	Head man.
Pathan . . .	A mixed tribe on the boundary between Afghanistan and Hindustan.

Peshwa . . .	Head of the Mahratta dynasty.
Pice	Small copper coin, one-half cent.
Poor	Town, used as a terminal, as Jeypoor.
Pujah	Worship.
Pukka . . .	Firm, strong.
Pundit or Pandit	A learned man.
Pundita . . .	Feminine of pundit.
Punkah . . .	A swinging fan.
Purdah . . .	A curtain.
Rajah	Prince or sovereign.
Rana	A prince or king.
Rani	Queen.
Rupee	About thirty-three cents.
Ryot	Peasant.
Saddhu . . .	An ascetic.
Sahib	Sir, lord.
Salaam . . .	Salutation.
Sari	Woman's garment.
Seer	Not quite two pounds.
Shabash . .	Well done.
Situra	A musical instrument.
Swami . . .	Religious teacher.
Tiffin	Lunch.
Tonga . . .	A light, two-wheeled vehicle.
Tulsi	Sacred plant.
Yishu Masib	Jesus.
Yogi	Hindu fanatic or ascetic.
Zayat	Wayside chapel.
Zemindar .	Hereditary occupier of the soil.
Zenana . . .	Apartments of ladies of rank.

AIDS TO PRONUNCIATION

a . . . Without an accent has the sound of *u* in *fun*. Hence many words are spelled for convenience with *u* in place of *a*, as *pundit* for *pandit*.

ai . . . Has the sound of *y* in *lyre*. Hence *Gosain* should be pronounced *Go-sine*.

e . . . Has the sound of *e* in *grey*. Hence *mela* should be pronounced *mey-lar*.

i . . . . Has the sound of *e*, as *i* in *police*. Hence *Bibi* should be pronounced *Be-be ; ghi, ghee*.

u . . . Without accent has the sound of *oo*.

TABLE

OF

CHRISTIANS OF INDIA

Official Returns of all India, issued from Calcutta, May 2, 1901

Total of all denominations	2,923,349
European and other races	258,990
Natives	2,664,359

	Total Returned	Natives
Anglican	453,612	305,907
Baptist	220,863	216,743
Congregationalist	37,876	37,313
Lutheran and allied denominations	155,455	153,768
Methodist	76,869	68,451
Presbyterian	53,829	42,799
Friends	1,309	1,275
Roman Catholic	1,202,039	1,122,378
Salvationist	18,960	18,847
Syrian	571,327	571,320
Scattering	131,210	125,558

INDEX